BREAKTHROUGH IN TIMES OF BREAKDOWN

By Marc A. Dupont

With Joel Kilpatrick

Beakthrough in Times of Breakdown

ISBN: 979-1-59352-536-1

Published by:
CSN Books
P.O. Box 1450
Pine Valley, CA 91962
1-619-445-1873
www.CSNbooks.com

Unless otherwise noted, all Scripture is taken from the New American Standard Version of the Bible.

Cover art provided by Sara Schultz.

Printed in the United States of America.

Table of Contents

About Marc A. Dupont

Marc A. Dupont has, since 1982, traveled extensively around the world speaking on the Person and things of God. He has ministered in a wide variety of conferences, denominations, churches, and leadership gatherings. He has authored a number of books including Toxic Churches, Pursuing Open heavens, Becoming the Friend of God, and has co-authored Healing Today. Marc and his wife Kim have three children.

About Joel Kilpartrick

Joel Kilpatrick is an author and journalist who has written more than fifty books, thousands of magazine articles and award-winning satirical humor. His work has been featured in Time magazine, the Washington Post, USA Today and many other outlets. He works with major publishers and ministers including Rick Warren, Mike Bickle, Bill Johnson and Michael Hyatt to help them communicate their God-given messages. Joel and his wife have five children and live in the Los Angeles area.

Foreword by John Arnott

I have known Marc Dupont for well over 20 years. He was the first to prophesy about the Toronto Revival. He saw it coming with the force of Niagara Falls, breaking the rocks and everything in its way. Sure enough, it happened as he foresaw, and less than a year later we were being overwhelmed by it. As a result, God has brought amazing breakthroughs around the globe, transformed millions of lives, filled us with His presence and revealed His Father's heart of love to multitudes. Now after over 20 years revival continues, yet we are living in a vastly changed Christian world. Mostly for the good, however the challenges are becoming greater and greater. This is a time when the wheat and the weeds are both reaching maturity. It is the best of times, and the worst of times!

Marc's timely new book, *Breakthrough In Times Of Breakdown* fills a vital and practical need in the lives of Christians today. He calls us to live in the promises and daily revelations of God to let vertical thinking and relationship with God guide us, rather than allowing horizontal opinions and rational thinking become our guide. In the Bible, Isaac sowed seed and reaped a harvest of one hundredfold during a time of famine. That was not a practical thing to do, but he listened to God and supernatural blessing and provision came. He heard and followed the voice of The Lord, and the miracle came.

God's ways are not our ways and can at times seem impractical. Yet when you hear Him and follow Him closely, it will always eventually lead to fruitfulness.

It really blesses me as one who loves and respects Marc, to see him grasping the powerful relational truths with God that release abundant blessing and fruitful ministry. The content and insights which he shares here are not merely bits and pieces heard and read, then cobbled together to present us with yet one more book. No, Marc is sharing, from heart knowledge and experience, truth that has been gleaned over years of faithfully serving God, all the while being loyal to his wife and family. His is a life well-lived with his Lord, his family and his friends. Well done Marc! I reflected and pondered my own journey throughout the entire book, agreeing wholeheartedly, and feeling stirred anew to seek first the Kingdom of God and His righteousness, so that all else is simply added in by a Father who loves His children.

So, you ought to read this book, yet more importantly, you need to revisit these truths on a daily and weekly basis, so as to implement them constantly into your life. This book will help you learn the ways and heart of The Lord and to experience His love for you. Then, entering into His peace, you can go forward full of faith and boldness, into your own breakthrough.

This book gives you the tools and the insights that you will need to finish well. Overcomers are then qualified to help facilitate breakthrough in the lives of others. This is fruitful ministry, and pleases the Father well.

-John Arnott
Catch the Fire,
Partners in Harvest, Toronto

ENDORSEMENTS

"God is still in the business of multiplying our little loaves and fishes when we offer them to Him. In today's world we need to learn that there is still a divine supply line. With joy, it is my pleasure to commend to you the strategic book full of wisdom, faith and brilliant teaching by my friend Marc Dupont."

Author of
Seer
The Lost Art of Pure Worship
The Lifestyle of a Prophet

James W Goll
Encounters Network, Prayer Storm
Compassion Acts

"Many Christians today struggle with fear and discouragement as they survey the world around them. This book is the perfect antidote to such negative thinking as it shows us how to be victorious even in difficult times. The Church has often made its greatest advances when faced with great challenges. The days of the early church were certainly such a time. This book shows us how to be more than overcomers as we keep our eyes on Jesus, our great Captain, and His wonderful promises to us. Every Christian will benefit by reading this inspiring page-turner. I will encourage every member of my church to get this book and read it. I hope it is widely circulated across the body of Christ.

This book shows us how we can walk in God's miraculous power and supply even amidst difficult times. In a time when many Christians have gravitated to extremes, this book demonstrates a refreshing balance and maturity. Churches and Christians will benefit greatly by following the biblical and mature path Marc lays out for us."

Mark Hoffman
Co-Senior Pastor Foothills Christian Fellowship,
El Cajon, CA

In this latest book, Marc challenges the modern-day Christian to not only be familiar with God's promises, but to also walk in them. As with most of his teaching, the book is full of moments where the God of Scripture suddenly reveals He remains Lord of today's difficulties. We read of miraculous healings, a liberating word of knowledge and inspired financial decision-making ushering in blessings. Faith grows by the word of one's testimony and Marc quite rightly challenges his readers to expect God's power, irrespective of difficulties, will accompany His promises.

Peter Thompson
Senior Pastor
Vision Christian Fellowship
Canberra, Australia

"If we grasp this teaching it will be personally life-transforming. If we live it out, our lives will radically impact the world we live in! These eternal truths, so articulately taught, full of practical application and threaded with living testimonies, will inspire, challenge and motivate the reader. Marc has brought this vital message to the Church at just the right time."

Clive W Corfield
Senior pastor, Father's House, Elim Church,
Lancaster UK
Founding director R.E.A.P

Dedication

I want to dedicate Breakthrough in Times of Breakdown to my wife, Kim. She has been my breakthrough partner for over 30 years now. She has been such a great source of love, joy, faith, and comfort to me. Especially during the difficult seasons she has truly been a woman who has believed God wholeheartedly for His amazing grace! Additionally, I would like to acknowledge the breakthrough faith I see in each of our children- Allie, Taylor, & David. I am so excited that as you have begun to face the challenges of adulthood each of you has chosen to 'trust the Lord with all your hearts' rather than simply lean to your own understanding.

Chapter 1

Vertical Thinking

The Bible is filled with promises of God — 3,000 of them, by some counts. That's pretty encouraging! But the facts "on the ground" are often quite different. Many Christians want to live by the promises of God, and perhaps believe that they are, but in reality they are failing to walk in those promises. Why?

The answer to that question is the subject of this book. Even in a time of breakdown, followers of Jesus are called to be people of breakthrough in every area of life, from finances to physical healing to personal peace. The worst times in the world can be the best times of our lives. The key is knowing how to walk in the promises of God no matter the situation around you.

Think of it this way. Most Christians are familiar with the promises of God and probably have a few favorites that mean a lot to them personally. But did you know it's possible to be familiar with something without ever experiencing the benefits from it? Consider a person who has never driven a car. Someone who grew up in a place like New York City might reasonably not need a driver's license because they get around by subway, taxi or bus. Every day that person would see cars all around him, zooming by on the city streets. He would see cars on TV and in movies. He would even ride in cars while taking taxis around the city.

But what would happen if one day a friend said, "I hear you're going to New Jersey. Don't take the bus; take my BMW and just return it when you get home."

The moment he handed over the keys to that nice car, the situation would be headed for disaster. Though literally surrounded by cars, the person would have little idea how to drive one. He might think as he approaches the BMW in its expensive parking stall, "Well, it can't be that hard. I've been watching people drive for years. I'll just do what they do and see how it goes."

Odds are he would bang that car up and hurt himself before getting it out of the parking garage.

That is the kind of life some Christians lead. They are surrounded by the promises of God. They read them in the Bible, hear them on the radio, listen to them on Sunday morning, study them in their devotional times and maybe even memorize them. But their lives are still beat up and hurting. They are familiar with the promises but not abiding in the promises. There's a huge difference.

Just as there is a particular way to successfully drive a car, there are also ways to successfully walk in God's promises. It is a learned skill. It does not come automatically. Just knowing the promises of God does not mean you know how to operate in them.

Moses knew this, and so he prayed a key prayer: "*Teach me your ways so I may know you.*" (Exodus 33:13, NIV)

He didn't pray, "Lord, activate Your promises in my life." Or, "Lord, I claim Your promises today." Rather, he sought to know the ways of God and how to walk in them.

Though Bible memorization is good, it's not enough to memorize Scriptures and hope that they will seep into our daily experience through recitation or even strong belief. We must learn God's ways of doing things. We must go beyond knowledge of God's promises to learning to live them out day-by-day. Then we will no longer have to pursue the promises of God; they will pursue us!

Triumph in Turmoil

I write these words during a time of great economic and social upheaval around the world. In once-stable cities of the West, protests and even riots are happening. Almost anywhere you look on the global map you find unrest, some of it violent. That anger is a result of fear, which can build up inside people and societies for years before shooting out like a cork from a bottle. Even people in the body of Christ are worried about the future, their retirement, what's happening in the Earth, what kind of society they are leaving for their children. This is the age we live in.

But a specific promise in Psalm 37:18-19 could enormously change our lives. It is a breakthrough promise designed for times when everything else is breaking down. It says that the righteous will prosper, even during a time of famine. Let me give you an example of this.

In my home country, the USA, a tremendous recession is underway. Unemployment is high. Many investors are not investing, so new jobs are scarce and many old jobs have disappeared. Poverty, drug addiction, violence and broken families are becoming more pervasive in American neighborhoods.

Yet three friends of mine, all business owners and manufacturers near my hometown in Ohio, have defied the trends. One friend owns a company that manufacturers plastic parts. Another owns a company that produces parts for airplanes. The third owns a company that manufactures files for working on horses' hooves. Each of these businesses is growing and expanding. While others are laying off employees and closing shifts, these three friends of mine are hiring employees, adding shifts and building bigger buildings. Why? Not because they are smarter. After all, they are friends of mine! How smart can they be?

The reason for their success is that they know the ways of God and are actively walking in them.

These friends practice one of the most basic ways of God which I call "vertical thinking." Everyone on the planet, Christians included, have a choice between thinking horizontally or vertically. Horizontal thinking is by far the most common. It means looking around us at the natural opportunities, wisdom and logic of this world. It considers earthly resources alone: human power, human abilities and anything we can see or perceive on our own.

Horizontal thinking is easy to recognize. It says, "If I seize this opportunity, maybe I can make success happen for myself. If I finagle this deal, maybe I can realize these promises."

That's how most of the world operates, but it's not how Jesus operated or how He called us to operate.

Even Christians fall into horizontal thinking. Someone may be truly saved and living a moral life, but still be trapped in a horizontal perspective. Perhaps they conclude that God has given us all the tools to make success happen on our own. Or maybe they do not see vertical thinking demonstrated around them. In any case, they look no higher than themselves and their circumstances for provision, with only an occasional cry to God for help — especially in a time of crisis!

Other Christians can speak knowledgeably about what Jesus did 2,000 years ago — the healings, miracles, Resurrection, parables and so on. Yet their everyday thinking remains horizontal. "What do I see? How can I make this work for me?" Horizontal thinking is the antithesis of what Solomon encouraged in Proverbs 3:5: *"Trust in the LORD with all your heart And do not lean on your own understanding."* (NASV)

Vertical thinking looks to God for everything: our provision, satisfaction, love, practical needs and our destiny. Vertical thinkers recognize that every good thing comes from our Father. Psalm 3:3 says, *"But You, O Lord, are a shield for me, My glory and the One who lifts up my head."* (NKJV) "Glory" means "the fascination of my life, the thing that occupies my mind." David is indicating here that he thought vertically. What captured his mind was the glory of God. His eyes were always on the Lord, the "One who lifts up my head." His eyes rose above the horizontal, earthly level into the heavens where true help comes from.

Jesus affirmed this principle by never talking about making believers but making disciples. Disciples go beyond familiarity to a practical heart knowledge of God and His ways. They learn to walk in the ways of God. That remains our calling today.

Paul said in Romans 12:2, *"Be transformed by the renewing of your mind."* (NKJV) He was pointing to the shift from horizontal thinking to vertical thinking. With horizontal thinking, nobody prospers in hard times except maybe the undertaker. With vertical thinking, anyone can prosper at any time as they set their eyes upon the Lord.

Vertical and Practical

My three manufacturing friends are down-to-earth people with degrees in accounting, engineering and such. They are not geniuses; they are better than that. They are vertical thinkers. They do not assess opportunities by what they see in the natural. Rather, they are people of prayer. They look first and always to the Lord Jesus Christ.

Here's an example of what that looks like in real time. A husband and wife who were in my home church, own a plastics company. They manufacture high technology plastic parts. They design and make the steel molds themselves for the injection molding process. They founded the business in 2002. Their ethos has always been not simply to ask God to make it profitable but to run the business according to His ways, values and leading. That includes making their decisions with the best interest of their employees at heart. In fact, they tend to see themselves as "shepherds" to their employees. This means praying with their employees, both Christian and non-Christian, when their employees are going through difficult times.

In 2009 they began to see great growth in their business, such that they had an opportunity to build a bigger building and take on more employees. At that time, they had six full-time employees working out of an industrial-type shed in their backyard. As business people, my friends knew they needed to expand the business, adding more employees and moving into a bigger building. If not, they would begin to lose ground. Horizontal thinking would have logically assumed that God was blessing them and that building a bigger building was the obvious next step. Horizontal thinkers might not have felt the need to even pray about the decision. They would have said, "Let's roll with this wonderful blessing and be faithful with the success God is giving us."

But my friends thought vertically. They didn't just go ahead and build a bigger building. They sought the Lord first and prayed, "Lord, we see an opportunity for growth before us. Should we move in this direction?"

Guess what? The answer was "no." Instead the Lord said to them, "Right now you have six full-time employees, and you pay them a pretty good wage, but you don't have very good benefits or insurance for them. Before you move into a bigger building and hire more people, I would like you to give better benefits and good insurance to your employees."

So instead of doing what a typical business might do, my friends invested in the employees they had. Although they were glad to be obedient to the Lord they felt they were probably setting back their move to a bigger and better building by three years. To their amazement, the employees got excited about the new benefits and began working harder and more efficiently. The company's output increased and they moved into a new building almost as quickly as they would have otherwise. The company got both things: expansion and blessing of the employees.

This is a very practical way of letting God be your "glory" and the lifter of your head. When He is your fascination, when your eyes are on Him, then His thoughts matter to you. You can literally implement His will in your situation, whatever your situation is. When it says He is the lifter of your head, it means much more than lifting your spirits so you quit moping around about your situation. To lift your head is to look to God and His ways. It's vertical thinking.

In 2010, my friends ended up moving from their backyard warehouse of 1,500 square feet into a new location with approximately 5,000 square feet. Due to their obedience to the Lord and the resulting favor of God on their lives they have seen their business increase by fifty percent almost every year, despite the U.S. economy doing poorly. Today, in early 2014, they are in a building of 26,000 square feet with more than twice the employees they had in 2009. Their building size today is more than seventeen times the size it was just five years ago!

Isaac the patriarch was a vertical thinker. In Genesis 26:1 it says, *"There was a famine in the land, besides the first famine that was in the days of Abraham."* (NKJV) We're talking famine on top of famine, years of little growth.

Isaac's response to the famine was not to panic, but to pray. He thought vertically and listened to what God would have to say. In response God instructed Isaac to relocate just some fifty miles away to Gerar. Verse 12 says, *"Then Isaac sowed in that land, and reaped in the same year a hundredfold; and the Lord blessed him."* (NKJV)

It's easy to breeze past a short passage like that without asking yourself, "How on earth did Isaac reap a hundredfold in a time of famine?" Many were, no doubt, living in despair and destitution, and yet Isaac never caved in to a despair and destitution mindset. He ended up investing in land, sowed into it, reaped a hundred times more and became wealthy.

What was his secret? Vertical thinking! He looked not at the parched land around him, but to the rich supply and wisdom that comes from above. He followed God's leading and did what may have seemed foolish, or haphazard, in the eyes of those around him, just like my friends did with their company.

It is important to note God's admonishment to Isaac found in Genesis 26:2: *"Do not go down to Egypt; live in the land of which I shall tell you."* (NKJV) Ancient Egypt, for the Hebrew people, usually represented trust in man and the ways of man. The prophet Isaiah rebuked God's people for habitually looking to Egypt and Pharaoh first rather than looking to God (see Isaiah 30 and 31). This almost always resulted in bondage and even slavery for the Hebrew people. In the same way we see a vast majority of the world today looking to the governments and "pharaohs" of our time for safety and deliverance rather than trusting God. All too often the result is slavery, in one fashion, or another.

Paul wrote that the things that we read about in the Old Testament are for our instruction (1 Corinthians 10:11). That means you and I are meant to reap abundantly in a time of famine! How? By thinking vertically and not taking God's opinion for granted. By giving Him first rights to every decision we make and everything we own. By humbling ourselves enough to learn His ways.

Psalm 103:7 says something interesting: *"He [God] made known His ways to Moses, His acts to the children of Israel."* Notice the difference? God answered Moses' prayer to know His ways while the children of Israel knew only His deeds. Do we have the same hunger to know God's ways, not just His acts and His power? Christians can read through the Bible and see the acts of God without ever learning His ways. We can become like the Israelites. They knew what God did, but Moses knew God's nature.

The Israelites took the taxi. Moses drove the car!

The ways of God are so different than we might imagine. The economy of heaven is never contingent upon the economy of man! God owns not just the cattle on a thousand hills, but all the gold, silver, diamonds, oil and everything else. He owns the universe. In a time of famine, He can cause the impossible to happen, because nothing is impossible with God.

The economy of heaven is based purely on God's provision and power. That's why Jesus advised, *"Seek first the kingdom of God and His righteousness."* (Matthew 6:33, NKJV) That's where the real power is! The favor of man may last for a season, but the favor of God lasts forever. We must walk with Him and in His ways. We should pray as Moses did, *"Teach me your ways so I may know you."* (Exodus 33:13, NIV)

God might have you do something completely different from what everyone around you is doing. Think of God instructing Noah to build an ark at a time when no one had even dreamed there could be a flood of biblical proportions! Your decisions may look foolish to people around you, but in the end you will reap a hundredfold, like Isaac did. It's called vertical thinking and it's based on the ways of God.

Vertical thinking works!

CHAPTER 2

Overcoming Identity Theft

To really understand this vertical relationship we have with God, we must realize once and for all that we have been adopted into His royal family. Each believer carries proof of identification inside of us; it's called the seal of the Holy Spirit. This reminds us that we belong to God's very own family. It is our primary identification, much more than our natural lineage, our country of citizenship or even our very name. The "least" believer in all the Earth is nothing less than a son or daughter of the eternal King and is entitled to whatever the King wishes to give to him or her.

A major problem in modern society has been something called identity theft. If you buy things on the Internet and the transaction is not secure, or give your credit card to the wrong store clerk and he or she uses it as if it belongs to him or her — that is identity theft.

This problem is actually ancient — it has been one of Satan's top strategies against the body of Christ for the last 2,000 years. He robs us of our identity. He convinces us we are not royalty.

In fact, the devil convinces people they are orphans, outside the blessing of God, when actually God calls us to sonship which means living out of the provision of the Father.

That is probably why the Apostle John was so emphatic when he wrote in 1 John 3:1, *"See how great a love the Father has bestowed on us, that we would be called children of God; and such we are."* (NASB)

Such we are!

Royalty is our reality. But is it realized in our lives? John was saying, "Understand this and never forget it!" He was fighting identity theft even in his own time. You and I have not just come into a different religious system, we have come into a life-altering relationship. Jesus Christ came and gave His life so that we could be restored to our Father, as it says in John 17:3. The whole plan of God is about mending a broken relationship between Father and children — and such we are!

Paul wrote something similar: *"For you did not receive the spirit of bondage again to fear, but you received the Spirit of adoption by whom we cry out, 'Abba, Father.'"* (Romans 8:15, NKJV)

Think of a child reaching up to his father and crying out, "Daddy!" Talk about a vertical relationship!

No matter your nationality or religious background — whether you were raised Buddhist, Muslim, agnostic, atheist or something else — when you gave your life to the Lord Jesus Christ you were adopted into the royal family. You are now a co-heir with the Lord Jesus Christ, according to Romans 8. You have been born into royalty. This is good news!

As a child of royalty, you have privileges that others do not have. Jesus made this clear in an interesting conversation with one of His right-hand men, Peter:

> *When they had come to Capernaum, those who received the temple tax came to Peter and said, "Does your Teacher not pay the temple tax?"*
> *He said, "Yes."*
> *And when he had come into the house, Jesus anticipated him, saying, "What do you think, Simon? From whom do the kings of the earth take customs or taxes, from their sons or from strangers?"*
> *Peter said to Him, "From strangers."*
> *Jesus said to him, "Then the sons are free. Nevertheless, lest we offend them, go to the sea, cast in a hook, and take the fish that comes up first. And when you have opened its mouth, you will find a piece of money; take that and give it to them for Me and you."*
>
> (Matthew 17:24-27, NKJV)

Jesus took this occasion to teach a lesson about what it means to be a son or daughter of the most high God. He essentially asked Peter, "Who pays the bills for royalty? The princes? The princesses? The queen? Of course not. The people do!" Royalty are exempt from taxes because they are sons and daughters of the King. When was the last time Prince Charles truly paid for anything?

As Jesus said, "The sons are free." Such we are!

Jesus actually lived out this principle in His earthly life. When He was born, the wise men brought Him quite a bit of gold. I believe that allowed Mary and Joseph to take Jesus to Egypt for a couple of years and pay all the bills. For a time, Jesus worked in His natural father's house, but as He walked into His destiny of ministry, He again stepped into the Father's supernatural provision and stopped paying the bills Himself. Why? Because He was the prince of the household. I think He still had wealth from those wise men, and we know He received contributions from wealthy families of His day (see Luke 8:3).

This also explains why, when the tax was due, Jesus didn't pay out of His "earthly" account but out of His Father's miraculous supply, via the mouth of a fish. God does not expect us to pay our way in the Kingdom. He supplies it all.

Covenant Supply

As a believer, all things are free to you in the Kingdom of God because you have a covenant relationship with God through Jesus Christ. You have come under the care and provision of your heavenly Father because you have come into His family. You are in covenant with Him.

What does "covenant" mean? It means a lot things, but let me give one simple perspective. In ancient times, people would come together and make a covenant of peace saying, "If someone attacks you, I will come to your defense, and vice versa." They would sacrifice animals, cut them up and put them in a pattern in the dirt. The two people would walk in a figure-8 in the midst of this bloody arrangement and say, *"May it be done to me what was done to these animals, if I do not fulfill my covenant promise with you."* (See an example of this in Genesis 15.)

What does that strange, ancient ritual have to do with Christianity? God the Father made a similar covenant with you. Jesus Christ, as the sacrificial Lamb of God, spilled His blood in the dirt as an eternal covenant sign of promise. He will not reverse it. The Bible says, *"God is not a man, that He should lie."* (Numbers 23:19, NKJV) He's never capricious or whimsical. There's never one day when He loves you more than the day before. That's the type of Father He is. He cannot deny Himself. He is in this covenant relationship forever by the blood of the Lamb, the Lord Jesus Christ. As a friend of mine puts it: "Covenant is the constitution of the Kingdom of God, and the Kingdom of God is the administration of His covenant with us."

That is why Jesus could say, *"For your Father knows the things you have need of before you ask Him."* (Matthew 6:8, NKJV) Jesus said He even knows the number of hairs on your head (Matthew 10:30). *"Therefore do not worry, saying, 'What shall we eat?' or 'What shall we drink?' or 'What shall we wear?' For after all these things the Gentiles seek."* (Matthew 6:31-32, NKJV) Gentiles were people outside the covenant.

God's covenant with you brought you into a vertical relationship with the King. We are free of horizontal thinking. You don't ever need to worry about the basic needs of life. Instead you can seek first the Kingdom of God. You are the King's kid.

Those who have surrendered their lives to Christ are now citizens of the Kingdom and beneficiaries of the New Covenant. We are free to be consumed by the love of God, rather than being mere consumers of things. We are free to be givers, not mere takers. This is why we can confidently state that "Kingdom living is in the giving." Our needs are met as we live in Christ and employ vertical thinking.

This fact frees us to use the money God gives us in a way that pleases Him. As we get to know His ways, we see that the first hallmark of His character and Kingdom is generosity. God never lacks, so neither do we. As children of the King we can be as generous as our Father. Indeed, He expects us to be. Jesus said, *"It is more blessed to give than to receive."* (Acts 20:35, NKJV) That is the nature of the King. That is the freedom that comes to the sons because we are looking to God, not ourselves, for our supply. When God nudges you, you can give sacrificially. God has even built in a principle that says that whatever you give, it will come back to you pressed down and in good measure.

A friend of mine grew up in a very poor Pentecostal family in the South. His father was a Pentecostal preacher at a little wooden church without a whole lot of people. Everybody was poor. Some even drove horses and wagons because they couldn't afford cars.

When my friend was five-years-old, his grandmother who lived in a distant city sent him a $1 bill. That was a fortune at the time, especially in the hands of a poor boy. He kept the bill like the prized possession it was.

One weekend his father's church had a well-known evangelist in to preach. Unlike the father who had a beat-up old car that barely ran, this evangelist showed up in a Cadillac. He wore a nice, white, 3-piece suit with an expensive handkerchief in the pocket.

During the service this evangelist took an offering and my friend said to himself, "I'm not giving anything." Normally he would throw in a couple of pennies, which was a lot for a kid back then. But he saw the evangelist's wealth and decided the man could do without a few extra pennies from a poor farm boy.

My friend left the meeting and was walking the dirt road home toward the farm. That's when the Lord said, "I want you to go back and give the evangelist your $1 bill."

"But, Lord!" my friend protested. "This man's rich compared to us. He has a big, new car, expensive clothes. Why should I give it to him? He doesn't need it!"

The Lord replied, "It's not because he needs it. It's about honor."

This boy fought the Lord on it, but finally trudged back and put his $1 bill in the plate. He was angry at God about it! He held onto that anger until he was a teenager and left the church for an alternate lifestyle. His heart strayed for a few years, and then he returned and has been serving God for more than forty years in evangelistic and prophetic ministry.

Many years later, this same friend was pastoring a church in Los Angeles and it was doing really well. People were being saved and healed, there was good cash flow and all indicators pointed to health. He showed up at the church office one day and an associate said, "Somebody dropped this off today." It was an envelope containing a check for $50,000 made out to my friend personally.

He was so startled by the gift that he went straight home and said, "God, I don't understand this. There have been a lot of times over the past twenty years in ministry when I desperately needed $50,000, but we had to pray and pray before it came in. What is this about? I don't really need it now. Why are you giving me this money?"

The Lord took him back to the memory of himself as a 5-year-old boy who gave $1 to honor the visiting evangelist. The Lord said to him, "I'm not giving this $50,000 to you because you need it. I'm giving it because I want to honor you because you've been honoring Me."

See how differently the Kingdom of God works? Even if you give a small amount, it comes back in better measure. You reap exponentially!

There is no need to be like those outside the covenant who are driven out of fear. We are actually prohibited from living in anxiety. Three times in the Sermon of the Mount Jesus commanded us not to be anxious or worried (Matthew 6:25, 31 and 34). It's not ours to think, "Oh, God, what's going to happen? Am I going to survive this ordeal?" Rather, seek first the Kingdom of God. Give, because that's better than receiving. In Philippians 4:19, Paul wrote that God will meet your every need according to His glory and riches in Christ Jesus. There are no limitations with God. He is in a covenant promise with you to meet your every need.

With vertical thinking we can be a breakthrough people even at a time when everyone else is breaking down. That's why it says in Psalm 91:7, *"A thousand may fall at your side, And ten thousand at your right hand; But it shall not come near you."* And *"though I walk through the valley of the shadow of death, I will fear no evil."* (Psalm 23:4, NKJV)

Why do I have a job?

You read this and say, "That sounds amazingly good, but that's not my experience. I show up at this stinking job, put in 50 or 60 hours a week and never seem to have enough money to make the budget work. What's the deal?"

The answer may surprise you. You have a job for two basic reasons, and neither one is to pay the bills. That makes absolutely no sense to horizontal thinking. Anybody in their "right" mind says, "Of course you have a job to pay the bills! Why else would you have it?"

There are two basic Kingdom reasons: First, a job gives you a sphere of influence. We can all admire the person who is called to be a missionary in some far-off country, or to start a church, or minister to street kids. But do you know that every one of us is called to be a missionary and ambassador for Christ? For many or perhaps most of us, that missionary work takes place at our work or school.

The number one reason you have a job is to have a sphere of influence for the Kingdom of God.

Some people get a job and the first thing they say is, "Oh, God, I'm the only Christian here! Maybe You don't want me here after all. Please help me to get a job where there are other believers!" That's horizontal thinking.

Here's a news bulletin for you: God has put you there to represent His goodness and grace. Who else is going to do it? Vertical thinking means thanking God for the privilege of being His chosen ambassador to the people around you!

As you represent Christ Jesus and pray for your job and co-workers, boss, the R&D team, the salespeople and CEO; as you speak words of kindness and blessing to your co-workers, not based on whether or not they deserve it but based on honor because they are a creation of God, you can change the atmosphere at your workplace. The Kingdom of God is much more powerful than your earthly situation. You can help usher in a vertical, Kingdom atmosphere and elevate others from horizontal, anxious thinking, just by acting like the child of God you actually are.

Jesus said the Kingdom is like a little bit of yeast that works through a whole batch of dough (Matthew 13:33). That tells us that a little vertical thinking and speaking goes a long way.

The second reason you have a job is to create value on the Earth. Our Father really does want to work on a day-to-day level through our labor, our company, our occupation. There is not one situation, product or business strategy that cannot be improved by vertical thinking. It doesn't matter how desperate or ugly things look. That just means the upside is that much greater!

If your idea of work is to merely show up and do as little as you can to get your paycheck, you are thinking with a horizontal, carnal mindset, not like a child of God. You are actually resisting what God wants to do in your workplace. Vertical thinking says, "Thank You, Father, for the job I have. How can I bless this company and our customers?"

God is a great businessman. Genesis 1:1 says The Earth was formless and void and there was chaos upon the land. Some theologians believe that was the time Satan was cast down from the mountain of the Lord and tried to wreak havoc on God's creation and future humanity (see Ezekiel 28:11-17). That may or may not be true, but it does say in the original language that there was chaos. Then the Holy Spirit began hovering in the midst of the chaos and God spoke light and life, totally transforming it. He brought healing, restoration, beauty and provision to a place of desolation and disorder.

That's a good job description for us. The Holy Spirit has not stopped bringing order, beauty and abundance where there is chaos. That includes at your workplace, school and neighborhood.

I mentioned my friend who owns a company with dozens of employees that manufactures files for horses' hooves. This industry is ancient. People have been filing horses' hooves for some 1,500 years or more. What could possibly be new about hoof files?

Several years ago my friend began to ask that very question: "Lord, is there anything new for tools for horses' hooves?" God gave him a vision and idea for a brand new type of file. There was nothing like it on the market. It took a year-and-a-half to develop and patent it, and now it's selling all over the world.

When we find ourselves in a dead-end mindset, thinking, "This is all there is. It will maybe only get a little better," we're not thinking with a vertical mindset. We're not allowing Him to lift our head so we can gaze upon Him. The Apostle Paul encouraged all of us to continually honor *"Him who is able to do far more abundantly beyond all that we ask or think!* (Ephesians 3:20-21, NASV)

There are no limitations to God's provision and creativity. He is the Creator of creativity! He has ideas for the oldest problems, the most mundane situations and even the things we barely notice. He is at work today as He has been throughout all of creation. Is He at work through you in your situation and workplace?

Speaking Vertically

So many times we find ourselves in situations where our only goal is survival. But God calls us to speak blessing and life through our prayers and public words. We are called to change situations because there is power and authority in the name of Jesus, the Name above all names.

Proverbs 18:21 says that *"Death and life are in the power of the tongue, and those who love it will eat its fruit."* (NKJV) You've probably heard this proverb many times. What, however, is highly interesting about this scripture is the fact that, in most translations of the Bible, the threat of 'death' precedes the promise of 'life'! God is all about life. Why speak of death first? It seems to me the writer is speaking a corrective word into our human condition: we are so prone to grumbling, complaining and criticizing. Before we can speak life, we must realize the damage that comes by speaking death. Whiners are not reflecting God and His Kingdom — can I hear an amen?

Paul listed grumbling and criticism in the same category as really "bad" sins like violence and immorality (see Galatians 5:19-21). Why? Because it took just ten men giving a bad report to keep 2.5 million people from coming into their destiny (see Numbers 13). They said, "The enemy is too big," and that report spread. People are so prone to grab hold of bad news and say with resignation, "As it has been, so it shall be."

Be careful what you feed your soul. The real news is not reported on CNN, Fox News or the BBC. The real news is the incredible advance of the Kingdom of God in our day! If you spend a lot of time watching and reading the news, make sure you spend at least as much time reading the Bible. There is so much pessimism and fear that if you allow it to, it will feed your soul and cause you to think horizontally.

We are called to bless and prophetically speak life. Jesus demonstrated this in the most practical way in Matthew 14:

> *As soon as Jesus heard the news of John the Baptist's death, he left in a boat to a remote area to be alone. But the crowds heard where he was headed and followed on foot from many towns. Jesus saw the huge crowd as he stepped from the boat, and he had compassion on them and healed their sick.*
>
> (verses 13-14, NLT)

Matthew tells us there were 5,000 men there. There were probably 12,000 to 15,000 people there at least, because they didn't count women and children in their crowd numbers back then. It was a desolate area — no shops or corner groceries.

People had been there for hours and were hungry. The disciples made a practical, compassionate-sounding request: *"This is a remote place, and it's already getting late. Send the crowds away so they can go to the villages and buy food for themselves."* (v. 15, NLT) Good idea, but not a God idea – they were thinking horizontally. They were not allowing God to be the lifter of their heads. They couldn't see what He was really up to.

Jesus said in verse 16, *"That isn't necessary—you feed them."* (NLT) With that, the disciples realized they weren't in Kansas anymore. They didn't even have enough sandwiches for themselves, let alone the masses. They were about to learn what I call the Loaves and Fishes principles.

#1 Bring it to Him

The first principle we see is illuminated when Jesus says, *"Bring them [the loaves and fishes] here to Me."* (v. 18, NKJV) Everything we have belongs to God. We have been bought with a price, the blood of the Lamb. We are stewards, not owners of everything we handle, big or small.

What do you have in your present situation? Whatever it is, the first step is the same: bring it to Jesus. Is your shortage in finances, wisdom or something else? Maybe you have a shortage of time because of your too-busy lifestyle. Maybe you are struggling because you feel your mustard seed of faith is not enough. Whatever you have, put it in the Master's hands. He will make good use of it.

Remember the account of the man who came to Jesus with the demonized son? Jesus was taken aback by the man's little faith. But this father did have enough faith to say, *"I do believe; help my unbelief."* (Mark 9.24) He took the little he had and surrendered it to Jesus. The result? A radical deliverance (spiritual healing) for his son!

#2 Relax

> *He then tells the people to sit on the grass (v. 19). They are not going to work for the meal of grace they are about to receive. This is our second principle: Relax! Every good and perfect gift comes from the Father of lights!*
>
> (James 1:17)

When people expect or desire a miracle, they tend to get all worked up. I see this many times when I'm praying for people. They assume the religious position (hands out, eyes closed, praying excitedly) and wait for the ka-boom. When they assume this posture, I often wait a moment. After a while they peek at me and say, "Are you going to pray for me?" I say, "I would love to, as soon as you get into a receiving posture."

You can't give and receive at the same time. Jesus had the people sit down so they were in a place of rest. You have an inheritance in Christ Jesus, and as nice of a person as you probably are, you didn't do a thing to earn it. Neither did I. We are co-heirs, sons and daughters completely by grace. We cannot strive for the Lord's love and provision. It doesn't come that way. It comes by relaxed faith.

#3 Break it up

Jesus then looked up (v. 19), allowing the Father to be the lifter of His head and demonstrating vertical thinking literally and figuratively. He said a blessing, gave thanks and broke the loaves.

Here's our third principle, and you may not like it: He broke up what he had. Some people need to take the money they have stored up in their various accounts and break it up a bit. We're not here to be consumers but to be consumed by God, His love and His purposes. We should always be taking what we have and "breaking it up" to feed and supply others. Imagine what this situation would have looked like if Jesus hadn't broken the bread and fish. No miracle, no food. In the same way, if you want a miracle you will oftentimes be called upon to break up what you have and give it away.

We all know the ending. He gave it out and nobody went away hungry. They took up baskets full of broken pieces and ended up with more than they started with because they took what they had and put it into God's hands.

#4 Bless it

Horizontal assessments of the little we seem to have often lead to grumbling, then to anxiety, fear, depression, anger and so on. Vertical thinking, on the other hand, fills one's gaze with the Father's endless resources which, when His love and our faith connect, all become available. This is why Jesus looked upwards and blessed the little He had in hand. He was confident, as we can be, of living in the Father's provision. God releases power when we bless rather than grumble. As Proverbs 18:21 states, *"Death and life are in the power of the tongues."* (NASV)

#5 Divine Multiplication

In thirty years of marriage and ministry my wife and I have never made tons of money, but we've always been blessed. Why? Because we have lived beyond our means. We have lived like children of God. I do not mean we have abused credit cards; we never have. But with every check, every offering we regularly put our hands on it and say, "Father, thank You for Your provision. This belongs to You. We're giving it back to You. Would You multiply this now so it meets our every need?" We always attempt to live out of a budget God directs according to His provision, rather than a budget based on our resources and understanding. To live out of the Father's budget rather than our own is how Jesus lived His life on Earth.

The very first words of God to man recorded in the Bible have to do with multiplication. *"Be fruitful and multiply,"* says Genesis 1:22 (NASV). God goes on to say *"Behold, I have given you every plant yielding seed that is on the surface of all the earth, and every tree which has fruit yielding seed; it shall be food for you."* (v. 29) Seeds never look like much — just a small piece of seemingly dead wood (a lot like the cross). However, as all farmers know, when you take that inconsequential-looking seed and plant it, water and nurture it, life will break forth. Some two thousand years ago Jesus hung on a dead piece of wood. He offered up His life as a "seed" offering and we can only marvel at the divine multiplication — the Church — that has taken place since that day.

As we take what God has put in our hands and give it away as God directs, it comes back multiplied and fruitful. This is why Paul wrote that God will not be mocked because a man reaps what he sows (see Galatians 6:7). As we sow to righteousness — the purposes of God — we will reap from God's divine storehouse of abundance. With a glad heart we can theologically and experientially take hold of Jesus' words: *"It is better to give than to receive"*! (Acts 20:35)

The loaves and fishes principle and vertical thinking work in everyday life. These are the ways of God, not basing your budget on what you have in hand, but on what the Father tells you to do. The key is in blessing what God puts into your hands and then giving it back to Him.

Every situation you find yourself in is waiting for God's redemptive purposes. He wants you to be the one who brings that redemption and transformation to your workplace, home, neighborhood and school.

We are the King's children. Let's act like it with joy, confidence and humility.

Chapter 3

Supernatural Peace

I started this book with the subject of least importance — money — and now we move to something priceless: perfect peace. Who wouldn't trade their fortunes and paychecks for a soul flooded with peace? As Proverbs 17:1 says, *"Better a dry crust eaten in peace than a house filled with feasting—and conflict."* (NLT)

3 John 2 tells us that prosperity of the soul comes before any other kind of prosperity. John wrote, *"Beloved, I pray that you may prosper in all things and be in health, just as your soul prospers."* (NKJV)

That means God wants to bless you in every area of life, but if you're not prospering in your soul then nothing else matters.

I can think of many great athletes of our time who have made hundreds of millions of dollars in earnings and endorsements. Many seem to have perfect marriages with picture-perfect wives and children and all the outward things that constitute the "good life." Many, however, end up with broken marriages and families. The problem is almost always the same — a secret life and a bankrupt soul. As their reputations and responsibilities increase, the fractures in their character become chasms that soon swallow their success. Fear moves in, as do addictions and dangerous behaviors. Soon it all comes crashing down, sometimes in a cascade of public humiliation.

It doesn't matter how much success, prestige, power or money you have in the eyes of the world. When your soul is not prospering, no other kind of prosperity matters. I can only imagine what it feels like to be some of these "successful people" when they are alone, without family and eventually without even professional success to comfort them.

Not long ago, Steve Jobs, the founder and primary innovator for Apple, Inc., died. Like many prominent athletes who have crashed and burned, he was arguably the best in his field by a long shot. Apple computers, iPads and iPhones have dominated the industry and the culture for more than a decade. Arguably, no business leader has done more to shape our everyday lives than Steve Jobs.

But ask people who worked with him what he was like. Despite being worth $5 billion and having all his dreams fulfilled, he was an absolute nightmare to be around. The people in his inner circle were scared to death of what he might do. He would yell at people, cuss them out in staff meetings and fire or demote them suddenly. Despite all his talent, innovation and creativity, one thing he didn't have was peace.

I'd rather be me than any "successful" person who has no peace. God's plan is that our souls would prosper, because if we don't prosper in our souls, nothing else really matters.

A Big Loss

Ten years ago my wife and I started hearing from friends about a terrific investment opportunity for ministries like ours.

A group of Christian businessmen had combined finances and an investment group was helping them to make quick, eye-popping returns. One friend of mine, who operates in a different financial sphere from me, made enough money in a few years through this investment group to allow him to start orphanages in Kenya and Ethiopia. We heard many stories like that. At one point there was more than $100 million in this investment group and all of it apparently going to build the Kingdom of God.

I resisted joining the pack for several years. Friends kept urging me to do it, pointing to the profits others had made and used for ministry, but my spirit didn't say "yes." Finally, the shimmering opportunity outshone my inner witness. I saw friends making lots of money and starting great ministries, so I vetoed the Holy Spirit's voice within me, took some of our hard-earned personal and ministry money and invested it with this group.

The first two investments went very well. In just three months we made significant profits. Then, on the third investment, we gave money and waited for word on how it was doing. We waited — no word. We waited some more. Two or three months later I got an email message from this group. It said, "Unfortunately, we have bad news for everybody. Not only has this particular deal gone bad, but the person we've entrusted to be our intermediate broker internationally appears to have stolen all the money."

I remember thinking, "This is not good, but everything I have belongs to God. He's bigger than my bank account or lack of bank account." I went to sleep, slept well, got up in the morning and had forgotten about it.

That afternoon another email arrived with more clarification of what was going on. I thought, "I'd better tell my wife." I went in and said, "You know all that money from our personal savings and ministry that we invested?" She said, "Yes. What's the latest word on it?" I said, "It's all gone." As best I remember, she expressed real frustration at first but the loss failed to drag us down or discourage us in any real way.

Two weeks went by and I didn't think much about it. Then I had one of those delayed "aha" moments, like when you're an hour down the road and think, "Did I leave the coffee maker on?" I thought, "I've just lost quite a bit of money for us. Why am I not more upset? How come I'm not really angry at these guys, especially the one who stole the money? Is something wrong with me? Am I losing my grasp of reality?"

The Lord simply said, "No. You're living with My peace." Maybe you have experienced a similar sensation of being in a bad situation and still being at peace. I should add that my breakthrough of peace was very much contingent on repenting to the Lord for failing to heed His voice. After all, it was His money we were stewarding!

This peace is exactly what Jesus was talking about when He said, *"These things I have spoken to you, that in Me you may have peace. In the world you will have tribulation; but be of good cheer, I have overcome the world."* (John 16:33, NKJV) My wife and I could very much have used that money, but it had no bearing on my state of mind. My peace was not attached to my bank account.

By the way, the person who stole the money is in jail, last I heard, but gets out soon and has millions salted away in a foreign bank account somewhere. I am certain he is not experiencing millions of dollars' worth of peace in his soul, because none of that money was his. I'd much rather be in my shoes than his.

The Prince of Peace

Am I saying it's a great idea to invest badly and lose a lot of money? No. I am saying that peace is a basic hallmark of life in Christ, even in bad circumstances. Paul wrote in Romans 14:17 that the Kingdom of God is not outward things like eating, drinking or (we might add) success in the eyes of men, but righteousness, peace and joy in the Holy Spirit. Even in the face of turmoil you should have a deep-down sense of well-being that no amount of money can buy.

On the other hand, people who lack peace can be lounging on the best beach in the world, with an iced tea in their hand and their toes dabbling the surf and still feel like they're in the middle of a war zone on the inside. I've heard it said, "Vacation is a state of mind." And how.

Peace is a part of the fruit of the Spirit, as Paul reminded us in his list of nine aspects of the fruit (see Galatians 5). When someone is really filled with the Spirit, the evidence is not just manifestations of spiritual gifts such as healing, miracles, prophecy and speaking in tongues, all of which are important for extending the Kingdom. If someone is filled with the Spirit, the first thing you'll notice is that he or she is experiencing life-transforming peace, an unmistakable sense of well-being rooted in the fact that God loves each of us to the point of giving His very best, Jesus.

In one of my favorite passages, Isaiah 9:6, the prophet says that a Son will be born and the government of God will be on His shoulders, and of His Kingdom and peace there will be no decrease. He gives this Messiah four titles: Wonderful Counselor, Almighty God, Eternal Father and Prince of Peace.

Peace is God's very nature. That's why when Jesus or angels visited people on Earth, their first words were usually, "Do not be afraid." Being startled and amazed is one thing, but there is no fear in peace.

We don't always know the answer to our dilemmas, but we can always know the Person who is the answer. Life and death are in His hands, which is why in the worst situations we still find ourselves saying, "It is well with my soul."

What is the fear of your life? Is it a fear of the future? Loneliness? Cancer? Diabetes? Are you in a great financial pit right now? We don't always know how Jesus is going to solve the problems, but we entrust ourselves to His wisdom and power at work in us. His perfect love casts out fear (1 John 4:18).

Peace rules!

Boldness

Peace leads to something you may not expect: boldness. Proverbs 28:1 reads, "*The wicked flee when no one pursues, But the righteous are bold as a lion.*" (NKJV)

Wickedness can look bold, boasting of its strength and power. But wickedness is like the house built on sand: it collapses quickly. Wicked people always have a heart of fear. On the other hand, righteous people may look meek and lowly — even powerless — but they are as bold as a lion. That's a result of inner peace, the prospering of our souls.

I know this firsthand because I grew up feeling a lot of fear. Why? Because my dad was brilliant! He not only had an incredible IQ level, but in his college thesis he helped write part of an IQ test, which was the gold standard at the time. He had a photographic memory. If we were talking about some subject, he would say, "Oh, yes. In 1962 I read an article in the *New York Times* about that. Let me tell you what this physicist said." My mother and father got great grades in school. On top of that, my dad had been on the football team and been a captain of the basketball team.

Guess who didn't get perfect grades and was not a great all-around athlete? Me!

The more I tried to measure up to my father's IQ, his grades, his photographic memory and his athletic prowess, the more difficult and discouraging life was for me. They say certain family traits skip generations, and if nothing else, I'm proof of that!

I did play soccer for four years on a championship team, but I usually did not start games. When we were ahead by a lot, they would let me play. I had to work really hard to show any success on the field, in the classroom and in any arena of life.

To add to the challenge, from the time I started first grade to the time I graduated from high school, we moved nine times, often in the middle of the school year. I was always the outsider, the new kid. I remember getting into fist fights on my first day of school just because I was the new kid on the block.

It wasn't until I started coming into a revelation of the Father's love for me that I understood that my well-being is not contingent upon my performance. I have not been given a spirit of fear but a spirit of adoption, the Holy Spirit, by which I can lift my hands and heart and say, "Abba, Father." Peace came from knowing I've been adopted into His royal family.

As that peace settled into my heart, I began to have greater boldness. I was no longer afraid. Peace led to action! Peace is not passive; it's an empowering of the soul that equips us for battle.

Can you imagine Joshua, the young man who had to step into the shoes of the great man, Moses? How was he ever going to measure up? How do you measure up to someone who stretches out his hand and the Red Sea parts? But Moses told him, *"Be strong and of good courage ... do not fear nor be dismayed."* (Deuteronomy 31:7, 8 NKJV)

That kind of encouragement gives us peace, where our boldness takes root.

Where does the boldness come from to do things you've never done? To start a business in a time of economic downturn? To quit a good career to work with alcoholics or street people, or go onto the mission field? To start a new relationship in spite of the pain of a divorce? To pray for someone's healing with a terminal disease? Boldness comes from peace.

Peace is not the sleepy, all-accepting state of mind people paint it to be. It is an invasive, overwhelming force that conquers everything in its way like floodwaters overwhelming a levee. It is an all-powerful, all-encompassing presence of the Kingdom that transforms lives, heals bodies and restores souls.

Total Victory

In 1 John 4:18, the apostle wrote that there is no fear in love, but perfect love casts out fear. The word "perfect" used here and in much of the New Testament is "teleios," which means "complete, 100 percent."

Peter said something similar in Acts 2:21 when he preached the gospel on the day of Pentecost: *"Whosoever calls on the name of the Lord shall be saved."* (NKJV) In the contemporary church we use the word "saved" to mean only free fire insurance, escaping the pits of hell. That's not what the Greek word means. It's "sozo" which means to be complete, mended like a seamstress mends a torn garment or a physician heals a sick person. When Peter was preaching the gospel the day the Spirit fell, he was saying that whoever calls on the name of the Lord will be completely well and at peace.

Not 90 percent, but 100 percent. Not almost — completely.

Peace is powerful. It knows no truces. Peace is not violent but it is relentless; it wins, takes over and allows no fear to remain. Peace is total, and it launches us into what God has for us next.

That's why Isaiah prophesied that the Spirit would be upon Jesus to heal the broken hearts and set the captives free (see Isaiah 61). That's why Jesus said, *"Let not your heart be troubled."* (John 14:1, NKJV)

Why? Because there's work to do!

Every believer is called to be a pioneer for the Kingdom of God. Every one of us is called to extend the goodness of God to co-workers, classmates, friends and family. Every situation in life requires His peace to function properly.

How do you pioneer anything if you're afraid of doing the very basics? How do you advance in power when it seems like you're barely hanging on in your present situation? What takes us from a survival level of faith to a more-than-conqueror level of faith?

It is the peace of God, which surpasses all understanding!

Maybe you've noticed the correlation that as wickedness increases in societies around the world, so does fear. Wickedness and fear always go hand in hand, as the proverb indicated. Any riots and outbursts of violence we see around the world reflect a deep lack of peace. This fear has increased even in the past few years. People used to say, "I have a future, a history with this company, a pension. I have something to fall back on." Now many of those fall-backs and pensions have been lost.

We can expect to see fear and wickedness rise together. The good news is that both are easily broken by the power and presence of peace residing in us by the Holy Spirit.

A few years ago I was speaking at a meeting at my home church when a man experienced a remarkable touch of the Holy Spirit that resulted in an amazing healing. I had spoken at the meeting about the Prince of Peace, Jesus. When we went into a ministry time I had a short word for this man that said in essence, "Tonight is your night." The man, who was fifty-something years old, testified a few months later that he had been radically set free from lifelong depression. He had been able to come off the anti-depressants he had been taking for more than twenty years.

A year later he testified, "I've been so thoroughly healed of lifelong depression that I can't even remember what it's like. My whole life is changed. I wake up excited, not fearful. I look forward to each day because I realize God is with me, He's for me and is more than capable of taking me through whatever happens."

This man literally could not remember what fear was like! Each of us needs to experience the Prince of Peace at such a deep level that fear becomes a forgotten, unrecognizable memory. It's complete, 100 percent. No treaties, no bargains, no divided-land deals. Total peace!

Similarly, in Darby, England, several years ago one man testified of encountering the Prince of Peace in a meeting and being delivered of depression. His wife testified that she had a new husband after many years of marriage!

Peace never stays put. It jumps the normal boundaries and brings miracles where we might not expect them. A number of years ago I was speaking at a series of meetings in Indiana. A man came up to me as we were praying for the sick and asked me to pray over a prayer cloth. His brother, he said, was waiting in the car. The brother had fallen away from the Lord, developed lung cancer from years of smoking and was scheduled to have a lung removed in a week or two. He had come back to the Lord and had come to our meeting that day, but was in so much pain that he could not get out of the car.

"He's been sitting there for three hours," his brother said. "I have this prayer cloth. Would you pray for it and we can take it out to him while you continue praying for people in here?"

This man, his pastor and I laid hands on a (clean!) handkerchief and said, "Lord, just like You did through Paul in the book of Acts, would you anoint this prayer cloth?"

The pastor and the man went out to the car, put the cloth on the side of the sick man's chest over the bad lung and prayed for him. A week and a half later the man went in for the scheduled surgery, but they sewed him right back up without removing the lung because the lung was already healed!

Interestingly, the doctors said that not only was the damage gone, but that they saw a bit of scar tissue on the lung as if there had been an operation. Dr. Jesus, the Great Physician, had been at work.

Peace passes our understanding!

One of the video testimonies we have collected is from a woman by the name of Mary Patel in London, England. She was in the hospital undergoing a bone marrow transplant to treat leukemia. Her daughter brought one of Mary's scarves to a meeting where I was ministering. We prayed that God would do as He had done through the Apostle Paul in Acts 19 when cloths that Paul prayed for were anointed by the Holy Spirit for miracles. Her daughter took that "prayer scarf" to the hospital and prayed for her mother.

After Mary fell asleep, she woke up and had a vision of Jesus standing in the hospital room wearing hospital scrubs! She was healed and was able to check out of the hospital far ahead of schedule. The prognosis was that if she survived the treatment she would have at most two years to live. Six years later she is still in great health.

Peace invades the troubles of this world, big or small. In the Sermon on the Mount Jesus said, *"Do not fear, little flock, for it is your Father's good pleasure to give you the kingdom."* (Luke 12:32, NKJV) He knows your needs before He asks. There's not one need in your life He is incapable of meeting at any moment.

God's ever-increasing peace will lead you into boldness such as you have never known.

Breaking Shame

Not long ago a man sent me an email sharing the experience he'd had at a conference I was speaking at in north England. At a certain point we were praying and ministering to people as well as preaching and teaching, and I felt the Lord tell me to break strongholds of shame over people's souls.

I define shame as "deep-rooted, illogical ill feelings and attitudes about oneself." Shame and guilt often go hand-in-hand, but they are two very different things. Guilt is recognizing you've done something wrong, like speeding or saying a harsh word to somebody. But shame is when you continually feel bad and unworthy regardless of whether or not you have done anything wrong. People who aren't guilty of anything can have such a bad self-image that they feel shameful about anything and everything. They always feel second or third best, and always want to prove themselves. When they do prove themselves it's never enough.

It can be embarrassing to respond publicly when asked to admit that you experience on-going shame, but thirty or more people came to the front. One of them was the man who sent me the email. He wrote, "I have lived with shame all my life. I even felt ashamed of standing up and confessing I had shame at the conference you were at, but I forced myself to do it. While I was receiving prayer I felt this intense heat upon my head. It was so hot that even when I put my hand to my head, it felt hot. I received prayer for five minutes, then went back and sat down. When I got up to leave that session, for the first time in years I had feeling in the bottom of my feet. I've had multiple sclerosis for years. When I walked out, for the first time in ten years I was able to walk without dragging my right leg. I didn't know what was happening. I was so shocked! I've waited this long to write because I wanted to be absolutely sure God was doing something. It took about a month but all of my movements have come back to me. I'm now completely mobile, not trembling or shaking. All of my motor skills have come back. All my symptoms of MS are gone!"

Not all MS or illness is rooted in mental or emotional problems, but in this man's life it seems that the muscle control and nerve disorders were tied to thoughts and attitudes of shame. When God broke that shame, all the symptoms that manifested as MS were gone!

That is what the Prince of Peace is all about. He's not simply about big meetings, lots of noise and that sort of thing. He's about changing one life at a time. God wants to break the unhealthy strongholds that may have come from a father or mother, a favorite teacher or coach who said you would never amount to anything. He wants to break strongholds that arise from our own personal failures. Peace always leads the way. It breaks through and brings a flood of victory. Isaiah 61 says He wants to give us beauty for ashes. Where you've got a spirit of fainting, He wants to give you a garment of celebration. He wants to take your mourning and turn it to dancing.

God wants to start a work of beautification in your soul and mine, as it says in Psalm 149: *"He will beautify the humble with salvation."* (NKJV) That is the work of the Prince of Peace.

What Kind of God Is This?

Nine years after our financial fiasco with that investment group I can look at the money we lost and say that, while it would be nice to have it restored, we have not missed it because God has provided for everything He has led us to do. We don't always know how things will work out, but we know the One who works them out.

Even more importantly, situations like that give you a real-time opportunity to feel and observe yourself living in peace. That roots us even deeper in peace and gives us greater boldness.

When my younger daughter graduated from high school we threw her a graduation party, which involved me attempting to bankrupt myself by feeding and hosting some 100 people in our back yard. After midnight, as my wife and I were cleaning up, my daughter asked if I'd met a certain girl she was graduating with. "She doesn't yet know the Lord, but I've told her about you because she has a serious clot in her shoulder-chest area," my daughter told me. "She's only 17 but she has to go to the doctor a couple of times a week because if that blood clot begins to move to the heart, especially at night, she could have a heart attack. She's scared to death of what could take place. I've told her that you see Jesus heal people and she's going to church tomorrow. Are you going to be there?" I said I would be.

The next day at church a perfectly normal-looking 17-year-old girl came up to me and said, "Mr. Dupont, I'm Taylor's friend. Would you pray for me?" I asked a lady from the ministry team to lay a hand on her and we prayed.

A week later I was in London. My cell phone rang. It was my daughter. She said, "Mom said I had to tell you what just happened. Do you remember the girl you prayed for last Sunday? She went to the doctor for her normal check-up and the doctor can't find the blood clot. She's completely healed."

God's peace touched that girl. No longer did she have to fear that blood clot getting into her heart or lungs. Peace breeds greater peace. It is ever expanding, pushing fear and darkness out of the picture. Isaiah prophesied that *"There will be no end to the increase of His government or of peace."* (Isaiah 9:7, NASV) His peace and His ways should be continually increasing in our lives, our families and our spheres of influence.

I got the news of her healing while sitting with friends in London. After talking with my daughter, our conversation continued and a friend posed a question in a way I had never heard. He said, "In Romans 8, Paul says we are more than conquerors in Christ Jesus. How do you define being more than a conqueror?"

I was stumped. I had never thought about that before. Why would we want to be "more than" conquerors? What could be better than being a conqueror? What did "more-than-conquering" look like practically?

The question bothered me for a month. I meditated on it, turned it over in my mind and finally came to this conclusion: to be more than a conqueror means that by the grace of God you have won the major battles of your own life and are now able to help other people fight their battles.

Do you see how peace leads to more-than-conquering? From that deep assurance of God's love and care for us, we are able to boldly fight battles on behalf of others and lead them into the victorious peace we are experiencing.

Jesus did this in Matthew 8 when He and His disciples were in a boat going on a journey. There arose a great storm on the sea, the disciples freaked out and woke Jesus up, and Jesus calmed the storm. It says that the storm became perfectly calm. It didn't just subside a little bit so that somehow they could scrape by and make it to a distant port, just shy of drowning. No, it became perfectly calm.

The disciples experienced peace after the storm was gone, but Jesus, the Prince of Peace had something much greater: a prevailing peace even in the midst of the storm. Peace is not just the absence of trouble; it is the basic, essential nature of His Kingdom at all times. Jesus is never afraid!

Jesus is the ultimate cure for anxiety, fear and depression. Whether the fear and depression are spiritual or physical — and I've seen the Lord heal people of real chemical imbalances — the result is the same. In John 16:33, Jesus said, *"These things I have spoken to you, that in Me you may have peace."* (NKJV) The devil says the opposite. He whispers the lie into the ears of our souls saying, *"As it has been, so it shall be."* But the Word of God says that there are more and better things for those who love Him than we could possibly imagine (1 Corinthians 2:9).

If you are walking in total peace, that peace will turn to boldness. You will have the privilege of watching it break out and change the lives and situations around you. Completely.

When the disciples witnessed Jesus replacing the raging storm with complete peace they asked one another "What type of man is this?" It was the wrong question. They should have asked "What type of God is this?" The Prince of Peace is who He is!

Chapter 4

Yours for the Asking

Like many people, I sometimes turn on the news and wonder what on earth our politicians are thinking. Sometimes I wish I had five minutes with them privately to understand why they make the decisions they do, and maybe give them a dose of my own opinions! Of course, most people like me don't really get those opportunities.

In truth, we get much greater opportunities.

The fact is, we have as much time as we desire with the Creator of the universe, and our time with Him can literally shape not only our own destinies but the destinies of nations and families. Prayer takes you into the center of the deepest reality of all existence. When you spend time in prayer, you access the very throne of God and can change history by seeking His face and agreeing with what the Spirit is saying.

Much is available to us, but the Apostle James said it well: often we do not have because we do not ask (4:2).

A Son Who Didn't Know His Father

In a time of breakdown, the last thing we want to do is discount the generosity, the loving heart, the magnanimity of our Father. So much is available to us: peace, provision, boldness, comfort, healing and much more. Will we ask for it?

Some of us live Christian lives, but we don't really understand what the Father has available to us. Jesus told a story about such a person who literally lived in his father's house but did not understand his father's heart or ways.

In this story, found in Luke 15, a very wealthy father had two sons. The older worked hard in the family business and contributed to the wealth. The younger seems to have wondered why he should keep working when they had so much already. So he went to his father and said, *"Would you give me my half of the inheritance now?"* In ancient cultures this meant, in essence, "Dad, you're as good as dead to me. I don't care about you. I just want my inheritance."

His father complied and gave him half the family fortune, and the son moved to a distant land. In today's terms we would say he wasted the money on drugs, gambling and prostitution. He soon bottomed out and was literally starving. Then he came to his senses and said, "How many of my father's servants have food to eat, but here I am starving?" So he made his way back home.

The son had a repentant heart. He wasn't intending to ask to be let back into the family but only to have a job. Before he had a chance to ask, however, the father saw him returning and went running to meet him. In that culture, a grown man would never be seen running in public unless it was a battle situation because it required him to tuck his robes up and expose his undershorts, as it were. But this father ran to embrace him, gave him a ring to represent authority, covered him with a robe which symbolizes the righteousness we have in Christ Jesus, and put new shoes on his feet which is the ability to walk in the goodness of God.

Then he threw a big party for him.

The story, commonly referred to as "the story of the Prodigal Son" is wrongly named, in my opinion. It should be called "the story of the Prodigal Father," not the Prodigal Son. Prodigal means "extravagant to the point of being wasteful." (You actually won't find the word "prodigal" in the story itself. It's not a Greek word but a Latin one.) The son had indeed been "prodigal" or wasteful with his family fortune.

But the real prodigal was the father who was extravagant with his love for his wayward son.

Of all the parables Jesus told, this one is probably the best picture of God the Father and His love. He loved us while we were still His enemies. That seems almost wasteful to us! Business people know what it takes to make a good deal. By those terms, God does not seem a very good businessman. He gave Jesus and He got you! But that's what love does. It is prodigal, extravagant, over-the-top.

At the end of the story we see the character I want to focus on in this mini-drama. The older brother, always consistent and hardworking, comes in and finds a party going on. Servants are bringing food, there is loud music and laughter. He asks one of the servants what is happening, and when he learns that his brother has come back, the older brother is so angry that he refuses to go in. The older brother had been faithful and brought increase to the family business. And this brother who had lost half the family fortune and brought shame on the family name came back and got a party!

His father entreated him: *"Son, you are always with me, and all that I have is yours."* (v. 31, NKJV) But the older brother refused to join in.

Neither the older son nor the younger son understood the father's heart, but the older son's ignorance and hardness of heart seem far more dangerous. It kept him from knowing his father's ways, and loving him. We can almost see the younger son on a trajectory toward restoration, coming to appreciate his father's grace because he experienced it first-hand. As Jesus said, those who are forgiven much love much (Luke 7:47).

But the older brother had what we call a religious spirit. His judgments were based on how hard he worked. The father said something to him that I find devastating: "All that I have is yours." It's something we must hear if we are to be breakthrough people: "You could have had a party anytime you wanted it. Everything I have belongs to you."

The older son was so caught up in doing the right things, dotting the "i's" and crossing the "t's" to make himself feel smug and successful, that he never asked his father for more. He completely missed who his father was. He was not experiencing the grandness, the compassion and mercy of his father's true heart. He did not live in a way that availed itself of his father's generosity.

He did not have because he did not ask. And he did not ask because he was ignorant of the father's heart of extravagant grace!

Refusing the Blessing

I was speaking at my home church and during the ministry time the Lord impressed me, "There's a woman here who is about 45-years-old. She has severe asthma. As a child she couldn't run and play sports, and at age 25 her asthma got a whole lot worse. She often has to go to the hospital for oxygen. I want to heal her."

I spoke this to the several hundred people present, but nobody came forward. I thought maybe I hadn't heard clearly, so we continued ministering to others. A moment later the Lord impressed me that the lady with that problem was there, so I said it again. Again, nobody came forward.

Finally, ten minutes later the Lord impressed me again, so I said it a third time, and this time a woman came forward. A woman on our ministry team led in prayer for her.

Two months later the woman who had responded sent me a testimony. "I've had asthma all of my life, just like the word that you had," she wrote. "When I was a child I couldn't run or play or get involved in sports. But when I was 25 and had my first child, my asthma got a whole lot worse and I often had to go to the emergency room, just as you said. It affected my whole life."

She continued, "When you first described me, I said to myself, 'Isn't that amazing! There's somebody else here just like me.'"

Think of that: the idea that this gift of healing could be for her, that God in His mercy and grace wanted to release her from bondage, didn't even occur to her.

It gets worse. She wrote, "When you said the word a second time, nobody came forward. I said, 'I bet that word's for me, but I bet God is really angry now that I didn't go forward, so I'd better not go forward. I'll be in trouble.'"

To top it off, when she heard the word the third time she thought, "Maybe God is angry at me, but if I don't go up He's going to be even angrier." So she relented and came forward.

Imagine! Her view of God, at least at that moment, was not as a good, compassionate Father. Rather, she thought He didn't want to give her something good, and would be angry with her for not responding quickly enough. This false perception of God is probably one that many of us need to be "delivered" from.

God was not angry with her. He loves that woman, and you and me, as the apple of His eye, His choice sons and daughters. By the way, for the first time in her life that woman was absolutely free of asthma. It has not come back.

Sometimes we do not ask for anything because like that woman, or like the older brother in Jesus' story, we really don't understand that the Father is prodigal, extravagant and even (if I can say it this way) "wasteful" in His love.

Have you ever seen a beautiful woman walking hand-in-hand with an ugly guy? A friend of mine, when he used to see such seemingly mismatched couples, always said under his breath, "It's either love or money." Assume that it's love. Love is obviously blinding! Love gazes upon the pleasing things, not the problems.

The Apostle John said that God is love (1 John 4:8), and He is completely extravagant with it. This is the nature of the Father.

Colossians 1:13 says, *"He has delivered us from the power of darkness and conveyed us into the kingdom of the Son of His love."* In Matthew 10:7-8 Jesus told His disciples to *"preach, saying, 'The kingdom of heaven is at hand.'"* (NKJV) This is the assignment of everyone who follows the Lord. Jesus said, *"This gospel of the kingdom will be preached in all the world as a witness to all the nations."* (Matthew 24:14, NKJV)

God is at hand! When Jesus told disciples He was leaving to return to the Father, Philip said, *"Show us the Father, and it is sufficient for us."* (John 14:8, NKJV) Jesus seemed almost hurt by the request and replied:

"Have I been with you so long, and yet you have not known Me, Philip? He who has seen Me has seen the Father" (v. 9)

Everywhere Jesus went He left happy, whole, exultant, loving people in His wake. He healed people, multiplied food, befriended the lonely and corrected the sinner but never with condemnation. He put on display the radical kindness and extravagant love of the Father.

The problem is that we treat Him like the older son treated his father: we do not have because we do not ask.

Modern Prodigals

I'll never forget the first time I prayed for someone with leprosy and the Lord told me to put my hands on her hands. I thought, "Lord, it'd be really cool if You'd give me a word of knowledge right now: is this leprosy contagious or non-contagious?" We are to operate in faith, so I did it regardless, and I didn't catch anything.

In Bible times, people with leprosy were forbidden from coming into villages because they might be highly contagious. Nobody could determine which kind of leprosy they had, the contagious kind or the non-contagious kind, so they all had to live in leper colonies, forever cut off from friends and family.

But a leprous man dared to come into a village because he was desperate and wanted to ask Jesus for healing. He *"knelt in front of Jesus, begging to be healed. 'If you are willing, you can heal me and make me clean,' he said."* (Mark 1:40, NLT)

Did you hear him "ask" just now?

I love the response: *"Moved with compassion, Jesus reached out and touched him."* (v. 41, NLT) Jesus put His hands upon the leper, the untouchable of that society, and the man received two healings: his skin was cleansed, and, even more importantly, the stigma of being an outcast was broken off his soul.

We could go through half-a-dozen passages where Jesus performed miracles or radical healings because He had compassion. Compassion is not feeling sorry for someone...that's sympathy. Compassion grips you and compels you to take action to help someone.

I remember in the early '90s when AIDS and HIV were relatively new. Nobody knew how contagious they were so there was a stigma even greater than there is today. It was around 1992 and I was at a church in Sweden where I had been a number of times. The pastors in this Swedish town were friends of mine. One day between sessions the pastor asked me to go with him to visit a guy who'd grown up in the church and was now approximately 30-years-old. He had fallen away from the Lord, gotten involved in an "alternate lifestyle" and contracted AIDS. He had just a month or two to live. He had come back to the Lord and repented of his lifestyle, but if the Lord didn't heal him he would die.

Did you know Jesus has compassion on people with AIDS, just as he did on lepers 2,000 years ago?

We went to his house. A woman from the church was helping him by making coffee and preparing food. He was so weak that all he could do was get from his bed to the couch. You could tell he didn't have long to live.

We sat down and had coffee. He told us his story, and then I said, "Let's pray and see what the Lord wants to do today." We prayed and I strongly felt the compassion of God for him. He was like the prodigal son who had known the father's love but run away. Now he was back and desperate.

We prayed for fifteen or twenty minutes. We asked for a release of God's goodness, power and compassion, and spoke healing to his blood and immune system.

Five months later I got a letter from the pastor. A few weeks after we had prayed, the man was in perfect health. He had experienced complete restoration.

God Loves Prodigal Sons!

A few years ago in Cleveland I was speaking at a conference. The pastor of this church had come down with non-Hodgkin's leukemia. We were praying for him and I said, "Anybody else who has an incurable disease, come up." Fifteen or twenty people came up. One guy was in his thirties. I'd never seen him and he didn't go to that church. I stopped in front of him and without knowing his disease I said, "The Lord is cleansing your blood."

A year later I got a testimony from him that was similar to the one from Sweden. This man had been in leadership in a church, fallen away from the Lord, moved to Miami, gotten involved with an alternative lifestyle and become HIV positive.

He repented, came back to the Lord, but was living on heavy medication and under a threat of death. When I had said that the Lord was cleansing His blood, he said he felt something come over him inwardly like he was being cleansed from the inside out. Immediately his energy levels went up. He saw his doctor and the doctor said, "I don't know what has happened to you, but all your numbers are normal."

For a year or more this man enjoyed perfect health. Then I got another email from him that said, "The symptoms of HIV have come back again. My immune system is weak, my energy low and my numbers are back up. What's going on?"

Healing is a mystery. God is the great "I Am" and we're the great "we're not." There's an awful lot that we don't understand about how He operates. Sometimes people are healed instantly. Oftentimes within a few hours or days, healing will kick in (see Luke 17:14). And sometimes symptoms come back.

Our job is to go on what we know: God hears our prayers; He is Jehovah Rapha, the Lord God who heals us. Psalm 103:3 states he heals us from all our afflictions. Sometimes that's instantaneous, and sometimes it takes time. In this man's case the symptoms came back after a year. My response to his news was, "I don't know what's going on, but let's fight the good fight together." You sometimes win a fight in one punch, but other times it can be like a war with lots of battles. War has setbacks but you can achieve victory if you keep fighting.

I invited this man and his fiancé to an upcoming conference as our guest. Something interesting happened there. Another speaker was demonstrating how to pray for the sick. Several hundred people were in attendance. The speaker said, "Who here has never been used by the Lord to release divine healing, but would like to?" Hands went up. He pointed to a mild-mannered middle-aged woman who came up to the platform.

This speaker said, "I want you to close your eyes and ask God what He wants you to bring healing for."

This woman freaked out for a moment! She saw all the people staring at her and didn't know what to do. The speaker said, "Just relax. Lord, give her a word of knowledge."

She quieted herself for a moment and then said, "I don't understand, but I feel like the Lord wants to cleanse someone of blood problems."

"Good," the speaker said. "Then pray for everyone here with a blood problem."

"How?" she asked.

"Just stretch your hand out and say, 'If you have a blood problem, be cleansed in the name of Jesus,'" he said.

She could have stretched her hand in any direction in this large meeting room. She could have made a sweeping motion to indicate everybody. But of all the things she could have done, she stretched her hand right toward our friend with HIV. "Oh, Lord Jesus," she said mildly, "heal people with blood problems."

"No, no, no," the speaker said, "That will not do. We are moving in the gift of faith here. You need to pray with authority. Pray like you believe God is cleansing people of blood problems. Say it again with all the authority you can muster, and if you don't feel authority, believe God has given you authority because that's faith."

She repeated much more loudly, "In the name of Jesus, be healed of blood problems!" Again she pointed right to my friend with HIV.

The first time she prayed, when she had said it mildly, my friend and his fiancé were looking at each other. The fiancé saw his whole countenance change. His face had been pale before, but upon that first "weak" prayer, color came back to him. His eyes got brighter; strength came into his expression.

When the woman prayed a second time, with authority, this man felt a jolt of electricity hit him.

I learned all of this later, because after that meeting I didn't see him for several years. Then I was in Boston at a conference and a guy walked up to me and said, "Marc, do you remember me?" It was him, but it took me a moment. When he told me his name, his story came rushing back to memory. I asked, "How are you doing?"

"I am completely free of HIV," he told me. "My blood is free of problems."

He received from God because he asked from God, and kept on asking!

Let me say in grace and love that too often Christians are like Muslims or Hindus in the way they exercise faith — that is, they are somewhat fatalistic. Muslims say things like, "If

Allah wills. If God wants to bless me with a good day, I'll have a good day. If he doesn't, I'm going to have a terrible day."

A few years back I was at a leaders' conference in Charlotte, North Carolina, and they brought up a pastor who was fighting cancer of the stomach. He said he had a year or two to live. As we went to pray for him to be healed, he said, "Well, if God wills."

I said, "No! That isn't going to cut it." Inside I was thinking, "Why am I more concerned for you than you are for yourself?" God tells us to seek, ask and knock! James said, "You do not have because you do not ask." If you're not going to ask, you're not going to receive. We prayed in faith and I felt the power of God present to heal, but I didn't follow up or learn what happened as a result. We just were obedient and spoke healing by faith at the leading of the Holy Spirit.

It doesn't matter if it's a major disease, an injury, or something comparatively "minor" going on in our bodies or our lives. God is a God of compassion and grace! He is the same in every circumstance — He wants to heal and restore. He is the extravagant, prodigal Father. He gives of His very best.

As we walk with God, we will experience the unbroken grace and mercy of the Cross. It doesn't matter if it's financial, physical, emotional or something else. It might even be something you brought on yourself, as with the men with HIV/AIDS who were healed. When we repent and cast ourselves on Him, God gives us wisdom to change our way of thinking and behavior. But He also works miracles.

We are dressed in the righteousness of Christ Jesus (Romans 13:14). We have not because we ask not. But those who ask will receive. God's promises are ours for the asking. Will you ask today?

Ice Cream!

I sometimes hesitate to tell the following story because I don't want it to be taken the wrong way. Some churches and Christians reduce their spirituality to "big houses, big cars and big paychecks." God's plan for us is much bigger than material stuff. It is better to give than to receive! Remember, Kingdom living is in the giving.

And yet, sometimes God just wants to give us ice cream.

I really like motorcycles. I like looking at them, studying them — and especially riding them. I rode motorcycles before I came to the Lord, then got saved and became "serious" about God, which meant leaving motorcycles behind. They represented something frivolous to me. Then God dealt with that religious spirit and I realized my appreciation for motorcycles wasn't ungodly and, in fact, was a good hobby, as long as it was not idolatrous.

When my future wife and I got engaged we began to pray for our future: our children, the ministry and other things we wanted. On that list I put a motorcycle, but not just any motorcycle. God asks us to exercise discernment, so I wrote down "Harley-Davidson." If you're going to have faith, you might as well have a lot of it!

My wife said, "That's fine, but we're not going into debt for a motorcycle." So we prayed that God would provide the money for one. We opened up what we called the Harley-Davidson savings account. When everything was paid for and money was set aside for savings, Third World missions trips and everything else, we put some of what remained in the Harley-Davidson account.

But inevitably I would go to Eastern Europe or Nigeria and the Harley-Davidson account would get robbed because we wanted to give to the work there. After fourteen years, there was almost nothing in it.

We moved from California to Toronto, Canada, and it so happened that a man in our church was in the business of buying and selling Harley-Davidsons and shipping them all over the world. Naturally, I felt led by the Lord to become good friends with this guy! His name is Wayne. He told me, "I can get you the bike you want used for a good price." I said, "What's a good price?" He said, "About six or seven thousand dollars." That was six or seven thousand more than we had in the Harley-Davidson account.

Soon after that I was speaking at a conference on the other side of Canada where some very prophetic ladies attended the host church. Between sessions I asked these ladies to pray for me and see if the Lord had something for me. One of them had an amazing word: "Marc, God really loves you. You don't know how much He loves you. God wants you to ask Him for anything you want and He's going to give it to you, to help you understand how much He loves you."

I took this really seriously and thought, "Lord, could this really be You?" I went back to my hotel room that night and prayed, "What should I ask for? More anointing to be a better servant? More wisdom? My wife would love that." But nothing seemed to fit.

At that time we had two young daughters. Near our home I would take them to a park with swing sets, a merry-go-round, a teeter-totter and other fun stuff. Across the street from that was a Dairy Queen. My girls loved the ice cream there, and I loved taking them there because of the looks on their faces and the excitement they got over having ice cream.

As I was praying about what I should ask for, the Lord gave me a vision of myself with my daughters at this little park. He said in the vision, "If you were to say to your daughters, 'What would you like? I can either take you home and cook you some broccoli, or I can take you across the street for ice cream,' what would they want?"

I responded to the Lord, "They would definitely want the ice cream." Just so you understand, we have always eaten rather healthy in our family...lots of fresh vegetables, salads, fruits and very little processed foods and sugars.

The Lord said, "Marc, even though the broccoli is better for them, when you take them to the Dairy Queen, do you enjoy watching them eat the ice cream?"

I said, "Yes, I do."

The Lord said, "You enjoy that because that's what I'm like. I enjoy giving treats to My children."

I got His meaning, and so I said, "Okay, God, I want the ice cream. I want the Harley-Davidson."

There was just one problem: Wayne was moving his motorcycle business out of Toronto to a location far away. I had a prayer window of two-and-a-half months, and I started praying like crazy. I got home, called up Wayne and said, "You know the bike I want. If you run across it, get it and I'll buy it." He said, "How much money do you have?" I said simply, "Don't worry about that."

Two months went by. Wayne was packing things up, having his bikes shipped to the new location, but the bike I wanted wasn't coming in.

In that same time period we had three or more people come up at my meetings, give me checks and say, "Marc, this is not for a Third World ministry trip. We're not sure why we're giving this to you, but the Lord has told us He wants to do something special for you." My wife and I both knew this was for the Harley-Davidson account.

The days dwindled down, and soon I was calling Wayne almost hourly to see if someone had brought in "my" bike. Finally he said, "The bike finally came in. It's incredible. Brand new condition. I could easily sell it for $8,000 or $9,000, but I'll sell it to you for what I paid for it: $4,500."

I had $3,000 in the account. He said, "The bike is yours. I'll trust you for the rest." Three weeks later the rest of the money came in miraculously.

When I first took that motorcycle for a ride, I realized, "This is a gift from my Father. I didn't manipulate this and make it happen. I didn't rush things and take out a loan for this." Many times I had prayed and the Lord had never said "no," but he never said "now." Until now.

God had given me the ice cream.

It is better to give than to receive — I believe that and live that. At the same time, there are times in your life when God wants to give you the ice cream. In the end, it's not even the ice cream that matters, but knowing in your heart how extravagant the Father is with His love for you.

We are breakthrough people by design. When we live in breakthrough in times of breakdown, we are experiencing that vertical relationship with our Father who makes all things possible. We were made to live according to His Kingdom and to have complete peace, complete provision and wholeness in every way. We are the sons and daughters of God!

So let's be people of breakthrough in everything we do and every area of life. Let's also bring breakthrough peace and power to those around us. With God's help, guidance and provision we can transform our world.

CHAPTER 5

More Than Conquerors

One of the ultimate questions Christians ask is, "What is God's will for my life? Am I called to be a missionary, a pastor, or something else? How can God use me in my neighborhood or job to make a difference in the lives around me? Does God have a spouse for me? What is my calling?" These are typical questions we all delve into at different points in our lives.

It is important to note that when the Bible, especially the New Testament, speaks about God's will for our lives it is primarily focused on who we are in Christ, not what we do in our work or where we live. God does lead us into specific areas of service. After all, God does all things well and with great intentionality and specificity. As David wrote in Psalm 139:16, *"In Your book were all written the days that were ordained for me, when as yet there was not one of them."* (NASV) He knows the plans He has for us and they are good plans! Plans to prosper the specific personality and gifts He has given each of us.

But His main priority is who we are more than our career or the other external facts about us. As with most truths pertaining to the things of God, it is the internal and unseen that impact the outward and external, not vice versa.

Creation Cries Out

Did you know that the whole Earth is actually crying out for you to become a breakthrough person? Paul wrote in Romans 8:19, *"For the creation waits with eager longing for the revealing of the sons of God."* (ESV) Your next-door neighbor who may be a Buddhist and your co-worker who may be an atheist both have a God-ordained hunger inside to know and see the person of Jesus, whether they recognize it or not. You are the one to show them! Jesus Himself is now seated at the right hand of the Father and you and I are His earthly representatives. We are the body of Christ! Creation and all the people around us are crying out for God to be revealed in us.

Paul continued, *"For those whom He foreknew He also predestined to be conformed to the image of His Son."* (Romans 8:29, ESV) God the Father has predestined that you and I should be living reflections of His only begotten Son, Jesus. This is God's will for you and me — that we grow up to Christ-like maturity so that people see Christ in us and through us. The specific "where's" and "when's" of life are less important than the "who" of our identity. This is why spiritual "identity theft" is such a major issue. If we aren't sure who we are in Christ, how will the world know who Christ truly is?

In God's way of thinking, situations shouldn't so much change us, but we should change our situations. Just as Jesus brought breakthrough everywhere He went, we are called to be His breakthrough operatives everywhere we go. We create value and bring influence of the Kingdom of God which enhances the quality of life around us. Just as God the Father looked at the formless void on Earth and spoke light and life into the situation, we can create value and release life into the situations where God places us.

My home church is extensively involved in ministering to low-income folks in our city. We believe in demonstrating the Kingdom of God both practically and supernaturally. One way we combine the natural and the supernatural is by taking bags of groceries door-to-door in impoverished neighborhoods. We greet the people and tell them we are there to demonstrate God's love in practical ways. We offer them groceries and then ask if they would like prayer for anything. The practical gift of groceries often opens the door for the supernatural gifts of the Spirit to operate.

A few years ago I had the opportunity to go out with a team to one such neighborhood on a Saturday morning. We went to several apartment buildings two-by-two. One team of men did not realize a certain building had already been visited by another team. So they loaded up and began going door-to-door there. As a door was opened into one apartment they could see that it was nearly empty of furniture. A mother and three young children lived there. When they asked if she needed groceries she burst out crying. Then she shared her story.

She was a single mom with no job and no friends or relatives nearby. She had just run out of money and food and had one week to go before her welfare check arrived. She had gotten up that morning, looked at the empty cupboards and prayed, "Lord, please send someone to me who knows You." In answer to her prayers she was visited by two teams that day and received a double portion of food and prayer.

That woman was crying out for a revealing of the sons of God.

Many years ago a friend and I were walking and talking in downtown La Jolla, California, on the Saturday before Easter Sunday. We were good friends and had not seen each other in quite a while and were catching up on what God was doing in each other's lives. We wanted a cup of coffee but the restaurants were still not open for lunch. This was before there were espresso shops on every corner. We wandered into a famous high-end hotel but the restaurant manager said they were not open yet. He invited us to sit at the bar where the bartender would give us coffee brewed for the staff.

As we sat at the bar with our coffees we noticed that the bartender was more and more overtly eavesdropping on our conversation. Finally she dropped all pretense of working and asked if we were followers of Jesus. She told us she had just moved from Florida where her neighbor had been sharing the Lord with her. This neighbor had prayed that she would meet Christians in San Diego. My friend and I shared our testimonies with her and prayed with her.

As we walked out of the hotel, three infirm elderly people were trying to get situated in their car. One was in a wheelchair, one had a walker and the other had a cane. We offered to help them in and then put the wheelchair and walker in the trunk. As we were about to close the car doors we told them we were Christians and often saw the Lord heal people. We then asked if we could pray for them for healing. They looked at one another and burst out laughing. They told us that they had just prayed together in one of their rooms that God would send someone to pray for them to be healed because they had no hope of healing otherwise.

These three travelers and the bartender at the exclusive hotel in La Jolla had something in common with the struggling mom with hungry children in Dayton, Ohio. Knowingly or unknowingly they were crying out for the revealing of the sons of God.

Jesus, the Son of God, was always about His Father's business. In fact, to do the will of the Father was Jesus' very *"food"* (John 4.34 NKJV). He thrived on doing the works of the Kingdom. Jesus said in the Gospel of Matthew, *"Blessed are the peacemakers, for they shall be called sons of God."* (5:9, NASV) The sons, therefore are the ones who by God's grace and power enable others to overcome hurts, hurdles and impossibilities in their lives. They impart and release the supernatural, life-changing peace of God as they walk with the Prince of Peace.

The Father's will for you and for me is that we reveal Christ to others in tangible ways. This means growing past a preoccupation with self and becoming "more than conquerors" just like Jesus!

More Than Conquerors

In chapter 3 I related how I had meditated on what Paul meant by the phrase "more than a conqueror." I came up with a working definition: "'more than a conqueror' means that by the grace of God you have won the major battles of your own life and are now able to help other people fight their battles." We see this in the life of Jesus time and again. Jesus won every battle He fought. Philippians 2 says that Jesus did not regard His equality with the Father something to be grasped, but emptied Himself and took the form of a lowly servant (Philippians 2:6-7). That tells us that He won the battle with temptation of selfishness.

Likewise, we see Jesus winning the battle of the three temptations in the wilderness before beginning His ministry. Finally we see Him in the Garden of Gethsemane winning the fight with the temptation of self-centeredness. What humanity lost in the first Garden through rebellion and disobedience

Jesus regained for us by surrender and obedience to the Father in the Garden of Gethsemane. What a wonderful symmetry!

Because He conquered the battles in His earthly life, He was qualified to conquer on our behalf at Calvary. Because Jesus overcame, He has been setting captives free and healing broken hearts for two-thousand-years all over the world. Because He is more than a conqueror He is now seated at the right hand of the Father who will give Him the nations as an inheritance.

We find this promise of overcoming also in the Book of Revelation. The seven messages Jesus spoke to the seven churches were each unique. But they had two things in common: the encouragement to the saints to listen to the voice of the Holy Spirit, and the promise of blessings to those who overcome. The rewards for overcoming included receiving hidden manna, receiving increased authority, eating from the tree of life, receiving a new name written in stone, and not being hurt by the second death. We are indeed called by God to overcome by becoming more than conquerors as Jesus is.

Three Levels of Faith

In our journey with Christ I see three levels of faith the Lord desires us to experience. The first I call Lamb of God faith.

Every person who comes into a living relationship with Christ Jesus experiences Lamb of God faith. Lamb of God faith is the simple but essential heart revelation that Jesus came to Earth as the only begotten Son of God and offered His life on the cross as a substitute for our shortcomings. John the Baptist and the Apostle John identified Jesus as "the Lamb of God"

(John 1:29, Revelation 5:6). This symbolic perception of Jesus was rooted in the Old Testament ritual of sacrificing a lamb for the people's sins on the Day of Atonement (Yom Kippur). The blood of a spotless lamb was sprinkled by the high priest on the mercy seat in the Holy of Holies. Jesus, as our eternal high priest, offered up Himself as a spotless sacrifice for our sins.

One cannot come into the Kingdom of God without this essential and foundational level of faith in Jesus as the Lamb of God. As Paul wrote, *"For by grace you have been saved through faith; and that not of yourselves, it is the gift of God; not as a result of works, so that no one may boast."* (Ephesians 2:8-9, NASV)

The second level of faith I call Jehovah Jireh faith. Jehovah Jireh is one of the names God gave Himself in the Old Testament. God stopped Abraham from offering up his son Isaac as a sacrifice, then caused a ram to become stuck in the thickets. In short, He provided the sacrifice for Abraham. Abraham then proclaimed the name of the place to be "the Lord will provide," or "Jehovah Jireh" in the Hebrew language (Genesis 22:14, NASV).

Many Christians live their whole lives from the narrow perspective that Jesus paid the price for their sins only so that they might escape the flames of hell and someday make it to heaven. They see the gospel merely as free fire insurance. But there is a whole lot more to God's love for us. As we grow in our knowledge of Him we begin to understand that He wants to be involved in every area of our lives. Although God calls us to work for His glory and live sacrificially, He also desires us to continually look to His grace and provision, not our strength and abilities. For this reason James wrote that *"Every good and perfect gift is from above, coming down from the Father of the heavenly lights, who does not change like shifting shadows."* (James 1:17,

NIV) Jesus said similarly that we are free to seek the Kingdom of God first because our heavenly Father is already committed to meeting our needs. He wants us to live in this reality every moment of our lives.

Living in Jehovah Jireh faith brings peace and security and enables us go from being takers to being givers, from consumers to being consumed by His love! Remember, Kingdom living is in the giving. Knowing God as Jehovah Jireh, our provider, enables us to live generously as a continuous, joyful lifestyle.

The third and greatest level is what I call Lion of the Tribe of Judah faith. John, the revelator recognized Jesus as the Lamb of God in the throne room vision recorded in the Book of Revelation, but he also understood that Jesus is the Lion of the tribe of Judah (Revelation 5:5).

Too many of us have a religious perception of Jesus as the eternal victim who innocently suffers for us forever. While we do need to remind ourselves of the Cross and rely on its power, we also need to be very aware that the tomb is empty! As the angels asked the women who came on the third day looking for Jesus, *"Why do you seek the living One among the dead? He is not here, but He has risen."* (Luke 24:5-6, NASV) Jesus is not the eternal sufferer but the triumphant champion of God!

You see evidence of this in the Old Testament when God instructed Moses to hit a rock with his staff to bring forth water for the thirsty Israelites. The second time they needed water, God told Moses to speak to the rock. Moses disobeyed and hit the rock with his staff again. God's judgment seems severe: He did not permit Moses to enter the Promised Land.

We might ask, "What's the big deal? It was only a rock. It's not like Moses committed adultery or stole gold from the offering. How could hitting a rock with a stick justify such a harsh judgment?" Because those rocks were highly symbolic pictures of Jesus, the Rock of Salvation. Out of Jesus flow the living waters, just as water miraculously flowed out of those rocks in the desert. The Father will only allow the Son to be hurt just one time in all of eternity, and that was at the Cross. Never again will the darling and champion of heaven be allowed to suffer!

Jesus is the victorious Lion of the Tribe of Judah who purchased by His blood people from every tribe, tongue and nation. He is the only begotten Son of God who will receive the nations as an inheritance. There is matchless power in His Name.

As we mature in faith and knowledge of God, we should reflect and release both the compassion of the Lamb of God and the authority of the Lion of the Tribe of Judah. In that Name is the power and authority for the miraculous, at the leading of the Holy Spirit. Demons have to obey that Name. When the Holy Spirit imparts the gift of faith there is even authority in that Name to raise the dead!

One of the testimonies featured on our web site is of a man who is now a U.S. Marine. Many years ago his father brought him to a meeting I was conducting in San Diego. At the time this boy was a twelve-years-old and suffered weekly with epileptic seizures. Many years later I found out that after just a few moments of praying that night in the Name of Jesus, the young man was totally healed. Years later when he went through neurological testing, the Marine doctors who knew of his history of epilepsy could not find a trace of that history. Praise God!

Lamb of God faith is our foundation for entering the family of God. Jehovah Jireh faith allows us to access the Father's Kingdom provision in our lives so we become givers and not takers. Lion of the Tribe of Judah faith allows us to believe and trust God for what is difficult and even impossible by human standards. As God said several times in the Bible, what is impossible for us is not even difficult for God. Paul, writing thousands of years ago to the church in Galatia, said that God not only gave them the Holy Spirit but did miracles in their midst (Galatians 3:5). Could it be that the reason many churches fail to experience much miraculous power today is that we have not yet matured into Lion of the Tribe of Judah faith?

The supernatural breakthroughs God has in store for us depend on His power manifesting in our everyday situations. Likewise, in order for us to be more than conquerors and facilitate breakthrough for others, we need to know the person of Jesus in our lives not only as Jehovah Jireh, who will meet our needs, but also as the Lion of the tribe of Judah. Then we can say with confidence,

> *Now to him who is able to do far more abundantly than all that we ask or think, according to the power at work within us, to him be glory in the church and in Christ Jesus throughout all generations, forever and ever. Amen.*
>
> (Ephesians 3:20-21, ESV)

Confronting the Realm of the Impossible

Recently a friend asked me how I would define God's miracles. I said that a miracle is "a creative display of God's power that accomplishes what is naturally, or humanly, impossible." I mentioned that one of the names God gave Himself in Abraham's day was "El Shaddai," which is commonly translated as "God Almighty." A better understanding of El Shaddai could be something like this: "The God who is able to do for you what you cannot do for yourself."

He is the God of the Breakthrough, El Shaddai, the Prince of Peace and the Lord who Provides. His name is Jesus, Yeshua, meaning "the Lord has become your salvation." To refer to yourself as a Christian is to identify with God Almighty who became our salvation. Just as our foundational breakthrough took place through the miracle of His resurrection, so miracles should be the believed and prayed for in the Church today. In the early church in Jerusalem, *"Everyone kept feeling a sense of awe; and many wonders and signs were taking place through the apostles."* (Acts 2:43, NASV) Likewise, we too should believe God for miraculous breakthroughs today. After all, God is the same yesterday, today, and forever. He is now and always the God who can do for you what you cannot do for yourself!

Remember the next time you feel surrounded by impossibilities that God may just be setting you up to experience the miraculous. And the next time you have the opportunity to serve someone who is surrounded by impossibilities you may just be the "more than conqueror" whom God has put in their path to release breakthrough.

The entire world is crying out for breakthrough. The only way it will come is through breakthrough people who are living reflections of Jesus, the God of breakthrough in times of breakdown. The prophet Daniel put it this way: *"The people who know their God will display strength and take action."* (Daniel 11:32b, NASV)

Let us be people who live out of Lamb of God faith, live with Jehovah Jireh faith and demonstrate Lion of the Tribe of Judah faith.

Let us be breakthrough people in a time of breakdown!

Let us bring breakthrough to others by God's amazing grace!

Amen!

Chapter 6

Epilogue

For Yourself — and Others

Being a breakthrough person will change your life for good. In fact, it will change your life for great.

If, for some reason, you don't feel compelled to become a breakthrough person for yourself, how about doing it for those around you? The people following your example in life? History shows that pioneers are the ones who open doors for others to follow. I believe God is calling you to be that person.

Consider the four-minute mile.

For decades, track coaches around the world worked hard with the best runners to break the seemingly impossible four-minute mile barrier. After trying and failing for so long, perhaps some leading coaches began to believe it was impossible. Perhaps the human body simply was not capable of pushing past the air resistance to run fast enough to complete the mile in less than four minutes, they may have reasoned.

Then on May 6, 1954, Roger Bannister of England did what they said was impossible. He ran the mile in 3 minutes and

59.4 seconds. Even more amazing is that over the next three years, sixteen other runners broke that seemingly impossible barrier as well!

Why did so many succeed so suddenly after decades of failure? Because of one person's breakthrough. Roger Bannister broke through not only the four-minute barrier but through the mindset of impossibility that had gripped even the best runners and coaches. He persisted and opened a door for others to follow. His success led to success for countless runners after him.

About a year before Bannister broke that barrier, on May 29, 1953, another epic barrier was broken. New Zealander Edmond Hillary and Sherpa Tenzing Norgay became the first men to stand atop Mt. Everest in the Himalayas. Many attempts had failed due to technical difficulty, bad weather and lack of oxygen. But since those two men broke through on Everest, more than four thousand climbers have gone on to do the same. Why? Because two men pioneered the path and paved the way for others to follow.

There are many other examples in athletics, medicine, finances, the arts and so on. But the greatest pioneer of all is Jesus who dared to walk the lonely, painful, shameful road of Calvary on our behalf. Many others had been crucified before Him. It's likely some of those crucified had been innocent of the crimes for which they were punished. Jesus, however, did the unthinkable. He chose to walk that road of death though He had never sinned. His pioneering breakthrough opened the door for millions to come into relationship with God the Father.

You may come from a family line that has been cursed by poverty, depression, alcoholism or other afflictions. Maybe marriages in your family line have been torn apart by divorce in each generation. Your family needs breakthrough. It needs a pioneer. Who is going to win that victory for your children, your grandchildren, your nieces and nephews, your spouse?

Why not you?

I meet many people who have no trouble believing for God's best for people around them but are themselves trapped by hopelessness. The lie fashioned in the pits of hell whispers that things will never change. That wicked idea gets woven into one's thoughts and begins to shape the future.

Don't you believe it.

God's idea for you, fashioned in heaven in the Father's very heart, is that His grace is infinitely more than sufficient to make you a pioneer, a breakthrough person, redefining generations after you. When the jailer of the prison in Philippi, where Paul and Silas were held, came to the saving knowledge of Christ it re-wrote not only his future but the future of his entire family. Is it any wonder the jailer was "filled with joy" (Acts 16:34)? He personally had experienced breakthrough and opened the door for his entire family!

Let me ask a pointed question: Is it possible that by inaction you could keep others in a jail of despair and bondage due to a lack of breakthrough vision? Are you stuck in a place of unbelief towards the victories God has in store for you? Let me encourage you to think of those around you and those to follow. Be a breakthrough for them. Let God open doors of freedom through your hands.

Jesus declared, *"The thief comes only to steal and kill and destroy; I came that they (you) may have life, and have it abundantly"* (John 10.10 NASV). Let's take God at His word and by His grace break through doors of impossibility. After all, God is for you, so nothing can stand against you.

Your destiny as a pioneer and breakthrough person is ready and waiting. Step into that destiny today!

Notes

Other Books by Marc A. Dupont

Becoming the Friend of God is focused, as the title indicates, on moving deeper into knowing the person of God as your best friend. Many know and refer to Jesus as 'Lord, and Savior'. As well, many understand that Jesus came to restore us to a vital relationship with God, the Father. Additionally many have learned to walk 'filled with the Spirit'- cognizant of the Holy Spirit's presence, leading, and empowering in their lives. How many, however, have truly learned that God is not only our Savior, Lord, and Father, but He truly desires us to know Him in a deep abiding friendship?

Jesus stated 'a better friend has no man than one who lays down his life for him'. Becoming the Friend of God examines four situations in the life of Abraham and how he responded so that in the both the Old and New Testament he is the only man God called his friend. This book is intended to help the readers realize how they can respond in similar situations so that they too might be called 'the friend of God'.

Healing Today, when the blind see and the lame walk is geared towards everyday Christians who desire to be used by God in releasing divine healing. Between the co-authors, Marc A. Dupont and Dr. Mark Stibbe, they have over sixty years of experience in not only praying for the sick themselves, but in training multitudes world wide in ministering healing in Jesus' name.

The book essentially has three components; One, the authors explain from a clear and basic Biblical position why God is in the healing business today and why He desires to use everyday Christians and not just the 'anointed superstars'. Secondly, the book identifies and outlines several different Biblical 'styles', or approaches of praying for the sick to help the reader learn that God uses us as we are, not religiously imitating others. Lastly, the book is chock full of testimonies the two authors have personally experienced that will impart faith to the reader that they too can be used by God, for signs, wonders and miracles.

Pursuing Open Heavens, was written to help believers in Christ live out a life of intimacy with God. Marc explores the whole concept of 'throne zone protocol' and what it means to live out David's 'one thing' prayer. As well, the book examines the Tabernacles of Moses, David, and Solomon and what those differences mean for Christians today who truly desire to know the reality of God's presence. If you are wanting to learn the art of intimacy with God on a deeper level this books may prove to be a valuable reference.

Toxic Churches, is the reprint of Marc's first book-Walking Out of Spiritual Abuse. Unfortunately, for some the good news can seem to become the bad news if their church life becomes poisoned due to the toxicity of insecurity, pride and ambition. Marc traces the life syndrome typical of some leaders who emerge into church leadership relying on outward anointing while trying to build the church on a personal foundation of wounds and brokenness.

As Solomon phrased it- 'one thing the earth can not stand is when a slave becomes king'! Marc, in a non-condemning fashion, examines the phenomena of when well meaning leaders, truly anointed by God end up hurting those they are called to lead. The book is far from a diatribe simply identifying the issue of spiritual abuse. Rather, it helps the possible victim correctly perceive what is, and what isn't spiritual abuse and then what steps to take if it is. The focus is on healing and restoration to grow and go on to living fruitful and fulfilling lives.

All of the above titles as well as many of Marc's CD's and Videos are available at:

www.marcdupontministries.org